PRAISE FOR *BLURRY*

"Very few introductions to biblical interpretation are at a basic enough level that you can hand them to virtually any adult Christian, including those brand new to the faith and to Bible reading, and have them be both helpful and understandable. Lokkesmoe has created precisely such an introduction. Plus it is short enough that interested readers should have no difficulty reading it in its entirety. Highly recommended."

—Craig L. Blomberg, Distinguished Professor of New Testament, Denver Seminary

"I knew this book had promise when Ryan compared the Bible to a Beatles anthology! His metaphors and analogies bring crystal clarity to an ancient text that is infused with Life. We are going to use this book in both our adult and student ministries, and I encourage you to do the same! This is simply a great book!"

—Pete Briscoe, Senior Pastor, Bent Tree Bible Fellowship

"Bible engagement is the single greatest catalyst to spiritual growth. Problem is, most people today do not know how to engage it. Just lying there on the table it is overwhelming and intimidating. Read *Blurry* and you will be equipped to see the Bible more clearly for yourself. And when you see truth clearly, watch out!"

—Randy Frazee, Senior Minister, Oak Hills Church, Author of *The Heart of the Story*

"What a helpful little book! If you're looking for a quick intro to the Bible that's both clear and interesting, this is it. You get the big picture of God's Word, as well as some memorable tips on how to read it. The discussion questions for each chapter also make this a fantastic choice for a small group curriculum. Highly recommend it!"

—Steve Gladen, Pastor of Small Groups, Saddleback Church, Author of *Small Groups with Purpose* and *Leading Small Groups with Purpose*

"Being a Kids' Pastor, I frequently interact with parents who desire to teach their children the Bible but struggle doing so because they themselves don't have a solid grasp on it. *Blurry* is a great resource for parents who want to understand the Bible and impart God's truth in the lives of their children. I highly recommend any parent to read it and then teach their children to use the techniques Ryan outlines in the book. Blurry has the potential to change the spiritual makeup of your entire family!"

—Jenny Jones, Kids' Pastor, Parkway Fellowship, JennyDayJones.com

"Nearly 75% of the people in our church are new Christ-followers or have been out of church for more than 5 years. For people who are new to the faith, *Blurry* clears up many of the confusing aspects of the Bible. Finally, a concise, easy to use, and clearly-written tool is available for those who need it most!"

—Mike McGown, Senior Pastor, Parkway Fellowship

"Whether you're a long-time Christian or just starting out on your journey, Ryan Lokkesmoe has put together a helpful and straightforward introduction to the Bible. I encourage you to read it for yourself and then pass it on to a friend."

—Larry Osborne, Author and Pastor, North Coast Church, Vista, CA

"We all know that reading the Bible is an important priority when it comes to feeding our souls. But the challenge for many of us is that it often seems a little 'blurry' and difficult to understand. But before you give up, let Ryan help you to turn the lens and bring scripture back into focus. Count on it, you'll be thankful you've read *Blurry*. It will empower you to open up scripture to both your head and your heart."

—Dr. Joseph M. Stowell, President, Cornerstone University
Grand Rapids, MI

"The Bible is the most amazing story of a God on the most daring rescue mission of history. In it, we find the story we have been swept into and the Author who started it all. Yet many of the people who sit in our churches don't turn to the Bible because they find it boring, irrelevant, or confusing. In *Blurry*, Ryan Lokkesmoe unlocks the beauty, mystery, hope, and redemption of the Story of God, and he makes it accessible and practical. If you want to ignite a passion for the Bible and give people tools for discovering it for themselves, Blurry will provide the corrective lenses we so desperately need.

—Heather Zempel, Discipleship Pastor at National Community Church
And Author of *Community is Messy* and *Amazed and Confused*

BLURRY

BRINGING CLARITY TO THE BIBLE

RYAN LOKKESMOE

CLC PUBLICATIONS

Fort Washington, PA 19034

Blurry
Published by CLC Publications

U.S.A.
P.O. Box 1449, Fort Washington, PA 19034

UNITED KINGDOM
CLC International (UK)
51 The Dean, Alresford, Hampshire, SO24 9BJ

ISBN (paperback): 978-1-61958-164-7
ISBN (e-book): 978-1-61958-165-4

Scripture quotations are from the *Holy Bible, New International Version*, ©
1973, 1978, 1984 by the International Bible Society.
Used by permission of Zondervan Bible Publishers.

Italics in Scripture quotations are the emphasis of the author.

ACKNOWLEDGMENTS

To Ashley: I cannot even begin to express my gratitude for all your love and support. I would never be in a position to write a book like this without your sacrifice during the first years of our marriage, and your constant encouragement and spiritual insight along the way. This book wouldn't be what it is without your helpful input and thorough feedback. Your fingerprints are all over it.

To Luke: I'll always remember writing this book as a new Dad. When I started, you were only a few months old. Now you're walking and exploring the world around you. I'll never forget the many times I was happily interrupted by the sound of your little voice. Maybe one day you'll read this book and get something out of it.

To Mom and Dad: Thank you for leading me to Christ when I was young, and for giving me your constant love and support through the years. You read many drafts of this book, and gave me such thoughtful feedback. You're my biggest fans, and I'm so thankful for you.

To Sean and Elise: Thanks for your love, support and enthusiasm about this book as well as for your willingness to read it and give me such helpful reflections. Your encouragement has meant the world to me.

To Grandpa: You and Grandma set a spiritual tone in our family that is now echoing four generations later in my son's life. Thank you for all the love, encouragement and Norwegian jokes.

To David, Christy, Holly, and Tim: What can I say? I started my life with one amazing family, and I married into another one. Thank you for your incredible support through the years, including taking the time to read drafts of this book. I can't say enough about how thankful I am for you.

To Mike McGown: Thanks for hiring a fresh-out-of-grad-school guy like me, and giving me the opportunity to be a part of the phenomenal staff at Parkway Fellowship. You have taught me so much about how to lead people and effectively communicate. I am thankful for your friendship, and the great blessing of serving under your leadership.

To the staff at Parkway Fellowship: What an amazing privilege it is to work alongside each of you in such an exciting ministry. I can't believe God allows me to serve Him with so many good friends. Y'all are the best!

To Mark Saunders: Thanks for roping me into joining the youth band at church all those years ago, and for spending the next six years showing me what it really means to follow Christ. I owe you a lot, my friend.

To Tom Eichem: Thank you for all the ways that you invested in me as a leader during college. I learned so much from your example. My years on staff in the High School ministry were some of the most fun, rewarding experiences of my life.

To Pete Briscoe: Your spiritual influence on me and my family cannot be overstated. Your sermons throughout the years laid a solid spiritual foundation and a sense of biblical truth that still guide me to this day.

To my educators: There are too many of you to thank individually. I owe a great debt to the faculties of The University of Texas at Dallas, Gordon-Conwell Theological Seminary, and the joint doctoral program at The University of Denver/Iliff School of Theology. Each of you brought the Bible to life in some way, and taught me how to think and write clearly about complex subjects. This book would not be possible without you.

To Dave Almack, Erika Cobb, Tracey Lewis-Giggetts, Sherif Gendy and the rest of the team at CLC Publications: Thank you for taking a chance on a young author like me, and for all your guidance over the last year. I'm honored to partner with CLC on this project, and I'm blessed by our shared passion for God's Word.

For Ashley

Table of Contents

1

BLURRED VISION

blur•ry \blər-ē\ *adjective.* Lacking definition or focus.
—Merriam-Webster's Dictionary[1]

When was the last time you saw a blurry picture displayed in someone's home? I'm not talking about an artistically out-of-focus photograph. I'm talking about something that is obviously meant to be in focus—like a portrait. Would you hang a blurry picture like that on your wall, or make it your online profile pic? I'm guessing no.

My wife and I take many photos, especially when we travel. We enjoy sharing pictures with family and friends and we make a habit of printing and displaying them in our home. I can remember many times when we thought we were taking an amazing photograph only to be disappointed later when it turned out blurry.

When that happens, we often don't appreciate the photo in spite of its blurriness. We don't show it to people. We don't print it and hang it on our wall. No matter how striking the object of the photo might be, we simply do not value a blurry picture. When things are out of focus, we just stop looking at them.

One Sunday morning at our church, I bumped into Kristen, a fantastic volunteer who serves in countless ways. Any ministry leader would want Kristen on his or her team because she is reliable, spiritually mature, and sets a great example for everyone who serves alongside her.

In the middle of our crowded lobby, I was talking to Kristen about some of our small group leaders, and the curriculum they were considering for their groups. Above the sounds of laughter and babies crying at the kids' check-in table, I told her that I had been encouraging these small group leaders to "keep it simple" and just choose a book of the Bible to study.

Kristen made a face. I can't even describe the face, but it wasn't one that said, "Great idea, Ryan!" She looked like she had something to say.

I stopped and asked her what she was thinking. Kristen had served with me in the Small Groups ministry for a while and I really valued her opinion. She started by saying, "Well [pause] don't take this the wrong way, but…"

Ok, time out. Don't you love it when people lead with "Don't take this the wrong way"? I thought to myself, "Alright, this is going to be good. . . not your superficial Sunday morning chit chat!"

Back to Kristen. She said, "Here's the thing. You always tell us to read the Bible more than anything else, and we *want* to. The problem is that we don't know *how* to read it. A lot of it doesn't make sense, and it's just frustrating."

I was surprised. I didn't expect to hear that from *her*. I thought to myself, "If Kristen feels this way, how does the average churchgoer feel? What about people who are seeking, or those who are new to the faith?" Kristen had given me the blunt truth about our church, and I suspect many other churches as well.

The Bible was blurry for Kristen and as a result, she didn't feel very motivated to read it. Since then I have searched for resources that I can recommend to people who feel the same way as Kristen – something that would bring some clarity to the Bible. I've looked for something that would be an easy first step for people who want to understand Scripture. Unfortunately, what I've found tends to be too lengthy, too comprehensive, or too complex—reinforcing the feeling that the Bible is for specialists.

Here's the real trouble: Bible reading among Christians is on the decline. I could trot out all kinds of facts and figures to prove the point, but suffice it to say that pastors, Christian college professors, and all kinds of ministry leaders have noticed the obvious decline in Bible knowledge over the last several decades. We've now arrived at a point where many of us have given up on reading the Bible altogether.

There are many theories as to why this has happened. For some, the Bible seems outdated—a book full of old-fashioned words like *thee, thou*, and *thine*. For others, it doesn't seem very applicable to daily life. For most people, the Bible is difficult to read and understand, which can be highly discouraging. It seems like a book for experts, and it's just simpler to retreat to the safety of other books, blogs or sermons.

It's easy to point fingers when trying to explain the decline in Bible reading, but that's not the point of this book, and it doesn't matter who is to blame. What matters is the reality we now face: Many of us have stopped engaging with Scripture, and it's often because we are frustrated with trying to understand it.

Imagine putting together a puzzle without having the picture on the box as a reference. You might get lucky and pick up a piece that makes sense on its own, but suppose you find a puzzle piece that just has a man's face on it. You can recognize that it is a man, but you don't know who that man is, what he's doing, why he has that particular expression on his face or why he's in the puzzle at all. That piece alone doesn't tell you very much.

Other puzzle pieces are only colors or random shapes. They don't make any sense on their own, and you have no clue what they are. You know that somehow all the pieces add up to a co-herent picture, but you have no idea what it is or how the pieces relate to each other.

That's how it is for so many of us when we read the Bible. It feels hit or miss. We might get something out of it, or we might not. There might be a verse here or there that makes sense, but what about the hundreds of other pages in the Bible? What do those pages say, and do they matter for my life? Is it worth the time to find out?

I grew up in church. I did the Sunday school thing, went to youth group—the whole nine yards. I memorized verses, learned the order of the books of the Bible, sang about how Zacchaeus was a wee little man and went on mission trips. Even with all of that, the Bible was always blurry to me. I struggled with under-standing it so I didn't make much of an effort to read it. I wanted to, but I didn't know where to start. The Bible didn't come into focus for me until well after high school. I can remember the moment exactly.

I was twenty-three years old and recently engaged to my wife, Ashley. We were in Europe doing short-term mission work with a couple of Christian ministries. While I was very excited to be do-ing ministry abroad, I increasingly felt like a spiritual lightweight because of my lack of knowledge when it came to Scripture. I had my Bible with me, and a seventy-nine-cent lab notebook I picked up from a drugstore. I was determined to find some way to read the Bible more seriously than I ever had before.

I was feeling some pressure too. The plan was for me to go to seminary after Ashley and I got married, and I figured I should probably know *something* about the Bible before I went. All cards on the table: This was my attempt at last-minute Bible-cramming before I went to seminary and met a bunch of Bible experts.

I didn't really know where or how to start, so I came up with a simple plan. I was going to read the Bible from the beginning and summarize each chapter in one sentence in my little lab notebook. I did it, and it worked! I was amazed at how God used that simple strategy to help me understand the Bible.

Forcing myself to summarize each chapter in one sentence required me to focus on that chapter and really think about what it was fundamentally saying. I call this strategy the *Single Sentence Summary*, and it's a technique I use today in my personal study of Scripture. Over the following five months we were abroad, I worked my way through almost the entire Old Testament. I can honestly say it was a turning point in my spiritual life because I finally felt the Bible coming into focus; it was much less *blurry*.

After that, I went on to seminary and learned more about the Bible. Some of it was fairly complicated and technical, like Greek and Hebrew, but a good deal of it was surprisingly simple. I found myself thinking, "How did I make it through a lifetime of going to church without hearing so much of this?"

Most of us, however, don't have the luxury to commit that kind of time or energy to studying the Bible or going to seminary. There is no lack of desire to commit to Bible study, but most of us just have busy lives. We struggle to find any time to read the Bible, much less study it in depth! We have jobs, kids, school commitments, financial stresses and countless other drains on our time and energy. That's just the way it is.

The aim of this book is to provide a concise resource that will help bring clarity to the Bible. I will not cover it entirely but instead will take a strategic look at four books: Genesis, Luke, Ephesians and James. Through the lens of these books, we will cover the basic story of the Bible. Actually, we won't even cover everything within each of these four books. We will focus on the broader structure and content of each book, and zoom in on a handful of passages to look at them more closely. We will focus on sections that get at the heart of what each book is about. In Genesis, we will learn about how sin came into the world and God's first steps to correct that problem. In Luke, we will meet Jesus the Savior – the ultimate solution to the problem we learned about in Genesis. In Ephesians, we will look at the nature of our new life that Jesus introduced to us in the Gospel of Luke. In James, we will get some very practical tips on how to live out the new life we discovered in Ephesians.

While exploring these four books, I will provide a handful of *Blurry Tips*—simple, memorable tools that will help you in your journey to better understanding the Bible. Don't feel the need to start using all of them right away. Just think about them. Notice the ones that make sense to you, and start applying those when you read the Bible. I have also included group questions if you are studying with family, friends or fellow church members. For easy reference, there is a list of all the tips on page 141.

We will also learn some basic information about the historical background of the Bible. God's story unfolded in real places at specific times, and understanding the biblical environment helps us to fully appreciate the significance of God's word. Hopefully, by the time you finish this book, you will feel the world of the Bible coming to life.

Four books of the Bible with *Blurry Tips* and historical insights along the way. That's it. No jargon. No cryptic diagrams. No incomprehensible theological speeches. This book is a straight-forward set of first steps that will hopefully propel you into a lifetime of reading and enjoying God's Word.

I concede that Genesis, Luke, Ephesians and James do not fully summarize the Bible, and that other writers might choose four different books. I also acknowledge that I could be accused of passing over vast stretches of Scripture that have a huge spiritual impact on the reader. This book is intentionally selective, however, and deliberately concise. My aim is not to minimize the complexity of scripture but to highlight the fundamental message of the Bible and provide some practical tips that can be applied to *all* of scripture.

It is my hope that after reading this book, the Bible will no longer be *blurry* to you. It is my prayer that God's Word will begin to come into focus, and at the same time become the focal point for you as you seek to learn more about God and grow closer to Him.

Group Discussion Questions

1. What have been the biggest obstacles for you in trying to understand the Bible?

2. Why is it important to have a basic understanding of the Bible?

3. What does society say about the importance of reading the Bible?

4. What Bible-reading strategies have been effective for you? What hasn't worked?

5. What do you hope to learn from this book?

2

WHAT IS THE BIBLE?

The first qualification for judging any piece of workmanship from a
corkscrew to a cathedral is to know what it is—
what it was intended to do and how it is meant to be used.
—C.S. Lewis, A Preface to Paradise Lost²

It's a simple question. The Bible—what is it? Some would say it's a book about Jesus. A book about Charlton Heston and those stone tablets. A manual for life. The basis of western civilization. The B.I.B.L.E.—Basic Instructions Before Leaving Earth. Don't you just love manufactured acronyms? Oh, and it's God's Word. The best-selling book of all time.

Surprisingly enough, the Bible is *not* a book. It might look like a book, and it might feel like a book. You can buy it in a bookstore. It sits on a bookshelf, maybe next to a bunch of other books. It has a table of contents and maps in the back. It looks an awful lot like a book—but it's not.

From a literary standpoint, the Bible is like an *anthology*. That's a word that we sometimes hear in the context of music. For instance, The Beatles are my favorite band of all time. My mom got me hooked on the *Fab Four* when I was young, and I never get tired of listening to them. I absolutely love their rich melodies and the musical range they showed throughout their career. If you listen to The Beatles' music from the early 1960's and compare it to something on their 1969 album, *Abbey Road*, it sounds like the music of two completely different bands!

Some of the most interesting Beatles albums are the *Anthology* records. They are compilations of famous Beatles recordings from different periods in their career, collected after the band had long broken up. Some of the tracks are live recordings, while some of them are studio tracks. Some of the selections are famous radio interviews or television appearances, like their performance on the Ed Sullivan Show in February 1964.[3] The *Anthology* albums span the career of The Beatles and showcase the evolution of their music as the most popular act in the world.

These albums are a great illustration of an anthology, a collection of previously unrelated things that are deliberately brought together at a later date to form a coherent whole. The word *anthology* has its roots in the Greek word *anthos*, which means *flower*.[4] It is the idea behind flower picking—going around and choosing what to include in a bouquet.

In the case of *The Beatles' Anthology* albums, all the recordings were done at different times and in different places throughout their career. They were not originally recorded with the intention of being collected together at a later date, but that's what happened. That's pretty close to what we find in the Bible, though we are certain God orchestrated the whole thing from the very beginning.

So even though the Bible looks like a book, it's not. It's an anthology—many books collected and bound together. It's like a miniature library on your shelf. This explains why it takes so long to read the Bible. It's not just a book, it's a whole library!

This is an important concept to grasp because, on a fundamental level, it changes the way we approach the Bible. It influences our expectations and the way we read it. The Bible is not one book written by one person at one time. It is a collection of books written by many different people at many different times in lots of different places. It's not just any anthology, it's a very *diverse* one.

Likewise, calling the books of the Bible "books" doesn't really do them justice either. They're not just books but various types of literature. Some of the Bible is poetry, some of it is history. Some of the books of the Bible are ancient letters written from one person to another or to a group. Portions of the Bible are made up of short, pithy sayings that help us to gain a bit of wisdom, and other books of the Bible are compilations of prophecies spoken by God's prophets. There is a rich variety of literature found within the Bible and calling them all "books" makes them sound pretty generic.

Add in the diversity among the authors, and we really start to see how incredible the Bible is. Some of the writings of the Bible were composed by poor prophets, others by wealthy kings. Some were written by spiritual leaders and traveling evangelists, while others were written by working-class people. The writings spanned hundreds of years and were written in places such as Rome, Greece, modern Turkey, Israel, and modern Iraq.

To acknowledge that the Bible is like an anthology is to acknowledge that God used variety to communicate His truth: a variety of people, in a variety of places and circumstances, through a variety of literary genres. This is the starting point for bringing the Bible into focus. When we understand that, we understand that not everything in the Bible can be read in the same way or with the same expectations.

This is also true for other content we read today. We read all kinds of literature in our lives and have completely different sets of expectations for each one. We actually read them differently because of those expectations, but we don't even realize we're doing it because it's so instinctive.

For example, if a book started out with "*Once upon a time…*" you would know you were starting to read a fairy tale. You would know that what you were about to read would be fictional, and would have fantastical elements to it. That type of story tends to be shorter, so you would probably read it in one sitting.

If you were reading a piece of literature that began with "*Today marks the end of a tumultuous week on Capitol Hill, with both Democrats and Republicans…*" you would know that you were reading the beginning of a news story. You would expect it to be primarily facts and would most likely read the article in one sitting.

If you started to read a book and the opening line read, "*In late 1941, the United States had yet to enter the war…*" you would know you were about to read a work of history. You would expect lots of dates and facts mixed with some analysis of the events. You probably wouldn't read the whole thing at once, but would stop at natural breaks in the story.

We read all kinds of literature in our lives and instinctively we know how to read each type and what to expect from it. The situation is the same with the Bible. Sometimes it feels disorienting to read one part of it and then go to another. We don't realize we've switched genres.

For example, you might be reading Psalms one minute, poetry, and then switch over to Galatians, a letter in which Paul is making a detailed argument and trying to convince his readers to follow his teaching on a subject. Those are two completely different types of literature! You wouldn't read a novel in the same way and with the same expectations as an email.

We're not going to cover every single variation of literature found in the Bible, but there are seven basic types: Historical Narrative, Poetry/Songs, Law, Prophecy, Wisdom Literature, Gospels and Letters.

Historical Narrative is just what you may think: a retelling of historical events in an orderly way. The book of Acts is an excellent example. It's a historical account of the first thirty years or so of the church. It's a pretty straightforward read.

Poetry and songs appear throughout the Bible, sometimes as whole books or pieces of other books. The Psalms are the best-known works of poetry in the Bible, but we also find songs embedded in historical narratives like the *Song of Moses* in Exodus 15. The Apostle Paul was even known to break out in song in the middle of his letters, like the early-Christian hymn found in Philippians 2:5-11. These passages use imagery, metaphor, and all the other types of artistic touches you would expect in a poem or song.

Law is found especially in the books of Leviticus and Deuteronomy and in portions of Exodus and Numbers. The Law was given to Israel so they would know how God wanted them to live as His people. It contains rules about many areas of life, as well as technical sections on temple procedures, sacrifices and purity regulations. Many people find the Law genre to be especially *blurry*, but there are incredibly valuable insights in these sections if you're up for the challenge!

Prophecy represents God speaking to His people through an intermediary, a prophet like Isaiah or Zechariah. Often prophetic literature is an indictment of the current state of affairs, and speaks about what will come in the future. There are entire books of prophecy, and just like Poetry/Songs, there are brief sections of prophecy embedded in historical narratives. A related type of literature is the *Apocalyptic* genre, which uses dream-like imagery and symbols to speak about the future. This is found most famously in the book of the Revelation, as well as in parts of Daniel and a few other books of the Bible.

Wisdom Literature is made up of teachings that offer practical life guidance. The book of Proverbs is the most well-known example of this type of literature, though much of Jesus' teaching would also be considered a form of wisdom literature.

The Gospels (Matthew, Mark, Luke and John) stand alone. Scholars actually debate how to categorize them because they don't fit neatly into any single literary category. The four Gospels, which describe Jesus' life and ministry, seem to be some combination of history and biography, with a generous amount of teaching and prophecy sprinkled throughout. They are unique.

Letters are precisely what you would think they are—letters. They are often written from one person, like Paul or John, to a church for the purpose of teaching and encouragement. But sometimes they are written from one person to another like Paul's letter to Philemon. The key thing to know is that these are real, ancient letters.

As far as the four writings we will cover in this book, Genesis is a mixture of historical narrative, prophecy and poetry. Luke is a Gospel, while Ephesians is a letter from an individual to a church. James is a letter full of wisdom literature.

The *Resources* section at the back of this book lists every book of the Bible categorized by genre. The main takeaway right now is that the Bible is rich and diverse. God used variety to communicate his Word to us. We shouldn't be confused by the diversity of what we find in Scripture. It was meant to be that way, and it's awesome.

DID YOU KNOW?

The early Christians pioneered a new technology in the first century: the book. You might not think of the book as "technology," but back then it was a major technological innovation. Before that time, ancient texts were written on scrolls. It took a long time for the reader to find the place in the text that he or she wished to read, and it was not easy to transport or store multiple scrolls without damaging them.

When the New Testament documents were being carried around the Roman empire, it was much easier to group them together in book format. The four Gospels tended to circulate as a group, and Paul's letters were often bound together. Being able to flip back and forth between pages provided several advantages, including quick referencing and ease of comparison. For example, the reader could easily flip from a passage in the Gospel of Mark over to a similar section in the Gospel of Luke. It would be a much longer process if they were written on separate scrolls.[5]

Group Discussion Questions

1. How would you describe the Bible in one sentence?

2. What does it mean to know that the Bible is not a "book"? How does this affect your view of God's Word?

3. What types of literature do you regularly read in your life? What expectations do you have about those types of literature?

4. Which type of biblical literature do you find the most interesting or challenging? (Historical Narrative, Poetry/Songs, Law, Prophecy, Wisdom Literature, Gospels, Letters)

5. What did you find the most interesting or challenging in this chapter?

3

GENESIS: PROBLEMS & PROMISES

When I consider your heavens, the work of your fingers, the moon and the stars, which you have set in place, what is man that you are mindful of him, the son of man that you care for him?
—Psalm 8:3-4

*I*n the beginning. These are perhaps the three most famous words in the Bible, and they kick off one of the most influential pieces of literature in history: the book of Genesis. Several of its familiar stories have made their way into pop culture like no other part of the Bible.

We are reminded of the beautiful scenes of creation painted on the ceiling of the Sistine Chapel. We may think of Adam and Eve frolicking around the garden of Eden wearing strategically-placed fig leaves. We may even think of talking snakes, apples and perhaps a hippopotamus or two lumbering up the ramp onto Noah's ark. Many people would be surprised to know that most of these famous biblical scenes come from just one book in the Bible.

The book of Genesis depicts God's creation of the universe, and the problem of sin entering that creation. It also describes God's initial steps to correct that problem and restore his relationship with humanity. It's an incredibly rich book, full of vivid imagery, sweeping historical narratives and prophecies that have been revealed throughout the centuries.

In this chapter, we will focus on a few highlights of Genesis. We will look at God's creation of the universe in Genesis 1 and 2, and then the incident in Genesis 3 in which Adam and Eve opened the door for sin to come into the world. After that, we will fast forward to chapter 12, where we will meet an ordinary man who was the recipient of some extraordinary promises.

Creation: Genesis 1 and 2

The book of Genesis starts out with a bang – not the unexplained, seemingly-random event known as the Big Bang Theory, but the deliberate, creative actions of an infinitely powerful creator.

> *In the beginning God created the heavens and the earth. Now the earth was formless and empty, darkness was over the surface of the deep, and the Spirit of God was hovering over the waters. And God said, "Let there be light," and there was light* (Gen. 1:1-3).

These first verses of Genesis are incredibly vivid and poetic. Can you picture this scene? Take a second to go there in your mind: *Everything is quiet. You can hear a pin drop, if pins had been invented. The Earth has no shape. It is formless. It is empty. Everything is dark. There is no light anywhere. There has never been any light anywhere.* Can you imagine what that must have been like? Even if we imagine the darkest and quietest place we have ever been, it would be nothing compared to this. We are looking at the blank canvas upon which God is about to paint His masterpiece.

Then all of a sudden, God speaks. With only *words*, He brings light into the darkness. Light did not exist before this. God not only brought light to the universe for the first time, He invented the *concept* of light. Nothing existed before this moment. Can you imagine how creative God must be to come up with the notion of light and dark? We can't even imagine a universe without light and dark. It's like trying to imagine a color that you've never seen, one that doesn't exist in our world. It's impossible.

When reading a poetic passage like this in the Bible, it's a good idea to slow down and allow the imagery to excite your imagination. Try to visualize it. Pretend the passage is a film. What would it look like? I find that reading the passage out loud or using audio versions of the Bible is very helpful with any kind of poetic literature. This helps me to not skim over the passage too quickly, and to really let my imagination paint a picture of the passage.

BLURRY TIP
When reading a poetic passage, slow down and picture it.

It's important to note that just because this passage is poetic and uses artistic language, it doesn't mean these events didn't occur as described. Historical events can be described in many ways, including poetically. For example, Francis Scott Key used lots of poetic language when writing the US national anthem, *The Star Spangled Banner*. Phrases like "twilight's last gleaming" and "rockets' red glare" artistically describe actual historical events, namely the Battle of Baltimore. No one would suggest that this didn't really occur simply because Francis Scott Key used poetic language to describe it. The same goes for Genesis and other poetic passages in the Bible.

Chapter 1 goes on to describe the creation of the rest of the world: the oceans, plants, sun, moon, animals and humanity. At several points in this chapter, God stops to look at what He has created and says that it is good. As you read chapter 1, the phrase "God saw that it was good" is repeated multiple times. It's important to pay attention to words and phrases that are repeated like this because they often reveal important themes or set you up to notice something later on.

BLURRY TIP
Pay attention to words and phrases that are repeated.

The final verse of chapter 1 summarizes the creation account by saying, *God saw all that he had made, and it was very good* (see Gen. 1:31). If you were to boil chapter one down into a *Single Sentence Summary*, it would go something like this:

GENESIS 1: SINGLE SENTENCE SUMMARY
God created everything, and it was all good.

In the second chapter of Genesis, God plants the garden of Eden and gives it to Adam. Everything has been created and Adam, the only creature made in God's image, has a place to live and work. Everything up until this point has been "good," but all of a sudden in Genesis 2:18, God says, "*It is not good for the man to be alone.*"

It's not good. Something is not good. After reading about all that was good in chapter 1, it's striking to all of a sudden see that God is calling something not good. In an otherwise perfect world, there is something out of sync. What comes next is God's creation of Eve—a wife for Adam. This shows us how much God loves us. He loved Adam so much that he was concerned about his feelings, and the fact that maybe he would feel lonely or unfulfilled on his own. He wanted Adam to experience a human relationship.

So we leave chapter 2 behind and everything is good. The whole creation is good, and the one thing that isn't good has been remedied through the creation of Eve. But something happens in chapter 3 that changes the course of history. So much so that we are still feeling the effects of that problem in our lives today.

The Fall: Genesis 3

In the third chapter of Genesis, we find probably the most famous single scene in the Bible: Satan disguised as a serpent, tempting Eve to eat the fruit from the Tree of the Knowledge of Good and Evil. This is the same fruit that God had specifically commanded Adam and Eve not to eat. Satan applies his usual tactics of lies, misdirection and rationalization, and Adam and Eve disobey God and eat the fruit. After they eat the fruit, their eyes are opened to the fact that they are naked. Adam and Eve hear God walking in the garden and hide themselves. When God calls out, they admit that they are hiding so that he will not see them naked. God replies with one of the most remarkable phrases in the Bible: "*Who told you that you were naked?*" (Gen. 3:11a).

Before they ate the fruit, Adam and Eve had no awareness of

themselves that would cause them to feel embarrassed or ashamed. Those feelings were not originally part of God's creation and His plans for humanity. So God wants to know why they are feeling things they should not be feeling. He already knows the answer, but he wants to hear them say it. God asks them if they disobeyed Him and ate the fruit, and Adam and Eve trot out the excuses:

Adam: "*She* made me eat it!"

Eve: "Satan made *me* eat it!"

You can hear God's heavy heart as He responds in 3:13: "... *What is this you have done?*" Satan had convinced Adam and Eve that they were just eating some fruit. No harm. No foul. But God knew that something incredibly significant had occurred. At the moment that Adam and Eve ate the fruit, sin came into creation. A perfect world was polluted. As a result, a deep chasm was fixed between God and humanity. God is holy and perfect, and things that are unholy and imperfect cannot be in His presence. This original act of disobedience changed everything.

Chapter 3 finishes with God banishing Adam and Eve from the Garden of Eden. The paradise of Eden was forfeited, and humanity would have to cope with living in an imperfect, sin-filled world. This event is commonly known as "The Fall."

GENESIS 3: SINGLE SENTENCE SUMMARY

Through the disobedience of Adam and Eve, sin came into the world and put distance between God and humanity.

In Genesis 3, comfort and closeness was replaced by pain and distance. More significantly, the perfect relationship humanity enjoyed with God was broken. God's most prized creation had turned its back on Him. To say that this was a problem is beyond an understatement. But God was not going to let things stay that way. God had a plan to get humanity back to where we started.

Meet Abram: Genesis 12

Centuries later, an old man named Abram was just minding his own business when God started talking to him. In Genesis 12:1-3, God said to Abram,

"Leave your country, your people and your father's household and go to the land I will show you. I will make you into a great nation and I will bless you; I will make your name great, and you will be a blessing. I will bless those who bless you, and whoever curses you I will curse; and all peoples on earth will be blessed through you."

Little did Abram know, he was at the beginning of God's intentional effort to repair the damage done in the garden of Eden. He listened to God, and he and his wife, Sarai, left their homeland and set out for the land of Canaan, the area of modern Israel/Palestine. A few verses later, God tells Abram He will give that land to his offspring.

God gave Abram two main promises: land and people. God intended on using Abram's descendants to build a great nation, and that nation would live in a particular land. Those are some big promises! Sometimes when reading a prophetic section like this, it's a good idea to make a numbered list of what has been promised or predicted. Otherwise, we can easily skip over some of the details and lose sight of everything that's been said. In this case, there are several promises in this one prophecy:

1. God will make a great nation from Abram

2. God will bless Abram
3. God will make Abram's name great
4. God will use Abram to bless others
5. God will bless those who bless Abram
6. God will curse those who curse Abram
7. God will bless all the people on earth through Abram

Wow! In this one short section, God has made seven promises to Abram. When you initially read the passage, it may not have seemed like seven promises. Again, making lists is helpful for understanding prophetic sections like this as well as the other types of literature in the Bible.

BLURRY TIP

If a passage contains a list, write it out and number it.

More On The Promise: Genesis 15

Abram and his family believed God's lavish promises, and they moved to this new "Promised Land" (that's why it's referred to as the Promised Land by the way—God *promised* it to Abram). After a famine and other struggles, God spoke again to Abram in Genesis 15:1-6, saying:

> *"Do not be afraid, Abram. I am your shield, your very great reward." But Abram said, "O Sovereign LORD, what can you give me since I remain childless and the one who will inherit my estate is Eliezer of Damascus?" And Abram said, "You have given me no children; so a servant in my household will be my heir." Then the word of the LORD came to him: "This man will not be your*

*heir, but a son coming from your own body will be your heir."
He took him outside and said, "Look up at the heavens and count
the stars—if indeed you can count them." Then he said to him,
"So shall your offspring be." Abram believed the* LORD, *and he
credited it to him as righteousness.*

So what's going on here? Doubt—like it would be for most of
us. Abram believed God's original promises from chapter 12, but
in the meantime, things aren't going so well. Abram is becoming
anxious. He thought he was going to have his own children, but
it hasn't happened yet. He was already an old man by the time
God made his promises, and he isn't getting any younger! Abram
is concerned that this other man, Eliezer, will have to inherit his
estate instead of his own promised child.

Abram wonders about God's promises and whether they will
come true. God decides to confirm His promises to Abram and
to illustrate them for him. He takes Abram outside and has him
look up at the stars. He challenges Abram to count them.

If you ever go outside the city to the countryside and look up at
the stars at night, it's breathtaking. You can look into space and see
the millions of stars burning bright in the universe. Trying to count
them would be foolish—there are so many it might as well be an
infinite number. That's what Abram is experiencing. He doesn't live
in a big city where the lights make it hard to see the stars. Abram
is basically camping with his family out in the desert. He is able
to see every star in the sky. There's no way he can count them all.

So how does Genesis 15 relate to what we covered in Genesis
12? Did God add anything new to the seven promises we listed?
Not exactly. In Genesis 15, God didn't make any additional
promises. He simply reaffirmed the earlier promises He already
made, and illustrated them in more detail.

BLURRY TIP

When a passage reiterates or retells something from an earlier
text, compare and take note of what is different.

Even More on the Promise: Genesis 17

A couple of chapters later, God gives Abram even *more* information about His amazing promise. In Genesis 17:4-8, God
says to Abram:

> *"As for me, this is my covenant with you: You will be the father
> of many nations. No longer will you be called Abram; your name
> will be Abraham, for I have made you a father of many nations. I
> will make you very fruitful; I will make nations of you, and kings
> will come from you. I will establish my covenant as an everlast-
> ing covenant between me and you and your descendants after you
> for the generations to come, to be your God and the God of your
> descendants after you. The whole land of Canaan, where you are
> now an alien, I will give as an everlasting possession to you and
> your descendants after you; and I will be their God."*

When reading the Bible, it's a good idea to get in the habit
of underlining or highlighting key words or phrases. This is especially true of longer passages like the one above. Not only do the
underlined portions provide a quick reference when you go back
and look at a passage, they also help you to be an active reader.
They prevent you from skimming over something too quickly.

BLURRY TIP

Read actively by highlighting or underlining
key words and phrases.

What information is new here? If you were Abram, what
would stand out to you? First of all, God tells Abram he will be
the father of "many nations." This sounds quite a bit grander than
the original promise in Genesis 12 that God would make "a great
nation" (singular) out of Abram. The scale of the promise appears
to be much larger than originally communicated.

If you were Abram, you certainly wouldn't miss the fact that
God changed your name. He changes Abram's name to *Abraham*,
the name he is known by to this day. The name Abraham is a
combination of the name Abram and another Hebrew word that
means "father of a multitude" (*Abhamon*). God chose a name that
reflected both Abram's name and the promise He made. Names
are often changed in the Bible when someone is called by God in a
special way. In this same chapter, Abraham's wife Sarai is renamed
Sarah. There are other instances of this in the Bible; for example,
Jesus' disciple Peter was originally named Simon.

The other new material in this chapter concerns the nature of
Abraham's descendants. Abraham now learns that some of them
will become kings! Also, the covenant (fancy word for "promise")
is described in this chapter as "everlasting." That eternal aspect is
a new element in the description of the promise.

After several chapters of historical narrative, God speaks to
Abraham one more time concerning His promise, and this time
it comes with a cost.

The Test: Genesis 22

Several years have passed, and God has begun to fulfill His promise to Abraham. His wife Sarah has given birth to a son named Isaac, a name which means "he laughs." God told Abraham and Sarah to name their son Isaac because they both laughed when God told them they would have a son in their old age.

Abraham loved his one and only son, Isaac. He had waited a lifetime for his son, and he loved him deeply. God knew that and decided to test Abraham. In Genesis 22:1-2, we read:

Some time later God tested Abraham. He said to him, "Abraham!" "Here I am," he replied. Then God said, "Take your son, your only son, Isaac, whom you love, and go to the region of Moriah. Sacrifice him there as a burnt offering on one of the mountains I will tell you about."

Did you catch that? God—the one who made the promise to Abraham to give him descendants—is now asking Abraham to kill his one and only son! Doesn't that seem just a little bit counterproductive?

Can you imagine how Abraham felt? The confusion and sorrow must have been overwhelming. He must have gritted his teeth and shaken his fist at God. He must have looked up to heaven through tear-filled eyes and *begged* God to change his mind. Despite this indescribable anguish, Abraham obeyed God and made the painful journey with his son to a mountain God selected for the sacrifice.

Abraham gathers the wood. He builds the altar. He watches his son Isaac's confused expression when he begins to tie him down. He looks into his son's eyes and sees the fear as he pulls out the knife. Words cannot express the agony Abraham must have experienced in those moments.

But at the last second, God stops Abraham. He has passed the test. Abraham has proved his faithfulness. Because Abraham is faithful and obedient, God says to him in 22:16-18:

"I swear by myself, declares the LORD, that because you have done this and have not withheld your son, your only son, I will surely bless you and make your descendants as numerous as the stars in the sky and as the sand on the seashore. Your descendants will take possession of the cities of their enemies, and through your offspring all nations on earth will be blessed, because you have obeyed me."

In the progression of the promises presented in Genesis 12, 15, 17 and 22, this is the final piece. God's promise will be fulfilled in Abraham and his countless descendants. They will be victorious over their enemies, and all the nations will be blessed through them. All of this will be true because of Abraham's faith and obedience.

Let's sum it all up. God created everything in the world out of nothing, and it was all good. Adam and Eve disobeyed God in the garden of Eden by eating the forbidden fruit. Because of this disobedience, sin came into the world and put distance between God and humanity. The relationship was broken. God was not OK with that, so he began to intentionally pursue humanity. He began to do this through his promises to Abraham, a man who would be the father of many nations and a blessing to the world. His descendants—some of whom will be kings—would live forever as God's people in the Promised Land. All of these promises were confirmed by Abraham's willingness to sacrifice his own son and the agony he experienced in the process. In this event, we see an example of God asking Abraham to do something He was ultimately going to do with His own Son, Jesus. It foreshadows

God's plan to restore the perfect relationship with humanity that He planned from the beginning.

DID YOU KNOW?

There was no apple in the garden of Eden. Despite countless paintings, stained glass windows and other literary works that suggest the forbidden fruit was an apple, there is no apple mentioned in the garden of Eden scene at the beginning of Genesis. The text simply says that Adam and Eve were forbidden to eat the "fruit" of a particular tree in the garden.

The Bible doesn't specify what type of fruit it was. It could have been an apple, or another common fruit from that part of the world such as a fig or pomegranate. Apples are only mentioned in the Bible about ten times. Figs are mentioned approximatley seventy times. So the numbers are in favor of a fig. Added to that, Adam and Eve made clothing out of fig leaves right after they ate the forbidden fruit.

Group Discussion Questions

1. What does it tell you about God that He wanted us to experience human relationships?

2. Which promises to Abraham were significant to you and why?

3. What does it mean to know that Abraham doubted God's promises?

4. What was significant about the way Abraham responded to God's command to sacrifice Isaac? What did you notice about God's response to Abraham's faithfulness?

5. What do you think of Genesis after having read this chapter?

6. Which *Blurry Tip* from this chapter did you find the most helpful and why?

7. What did you find the most interesting or challenging in this chapter?

8. What questions do you have about Genesis and how do you plan on finding the answers?

4

THE REST OF THE OLD TESTAMENT

*So there is hope for your future," declares the L*ORD*.
"Your children will return to their own land."*
— Jeremiah 31:17

If God made His promises to Abraham around 2000 BC, what happened in the next two millennia before Christ was born? That's quite a bit of time, and there's so much of the Old Testament left before you hit the New Testament.

It's important that we have a sense of the entire Old Testament story before we move on. This short chapter will be a glance at the rest of the Old Testament. It's just a glimpse so we have our bearings before we move on to the New Testament.

Please note: We are not skipping this much of the Old Testament because it's not important. We are not skipping it because it was invalidated or made obsolete by the coming of Christ in the New Testament. That could not be further from the truth.

The value of the Old Testament for Christians is proven by the fact that every single New Testament author quoted or alluded to the Old Testament in some way. In many cases, they quoted the Old Testament extensively as the basis of everything they said. One of my seminary professors, Dr. Roy Ciampa, used to say, "Paul isn't making this up!"[6] That was his way of reminding his students that almost everything the Apostle Paul said was based in some way on the Old Testament. Jesus and all the Christian leaders in the New Testament viewed the Old Testament as a critical part of their spiritual lives, and it remains so today.

You are reading this book because you desire to be equipped to read and enjoy the entire Bible. With that said, let's get a sense of what happens in the rest of the Old Testament.

Highlight Reel of the Old Testament

After God began to fulfill his promise to Abraham and Sarah by giving them a son, Isaac, God's promise continued to be fulfilled in the coming generations. When there was a famine in the Promised Land, Abraham's grandson Jacob and great grandchildren moved to Egypt where there was food. They stayed for many generations and multiplied exponentially. Abraham's descendants came to be known as the Israelites—God's people. You can read about the first few generations of Abraham's family in the rest of Genesis.

One day, a new Egyptian Pharaoh decided he didn't like all of these Israelites living in Egypt. There were too many of them, so he decided that they were going to be his slaves. There was work to do, and he figured they were just the people to do it. The Egyptians enslaved all of the Israelites, and the future looked dim for Abraham's descendants. But God remembered his promise to Abraham and felt pity for the Israelites. He chose an Israelite named Moses to confront the Pharaoh and dramatically lead the Israelites out of slavery in Egypt. After a number of miracles, including the famous parting of the Red Sea, God rescued the Israelites from captivity through the leadership of Moses. This probably occurred somewhere around 1400 BC. The escape from Egypt is depicted in Exodus 1-15.

After their rescue from slavery, the Israelites spent several decades wandering in the desert. They were no longer in Egypt, but they hadn't yet returned to the Promised Land. During this time, God gave the Israelites His Law, which taught them how to live as His people. This law included the Ten Commandments. There were thousands and thousands of Israelites camped out in the wilderness with God dwelling in their midst in a portable temple called the Tabernacle. Basically, it was a fancy tent. You can read about God's law and the Israelites wandering through the desert in Exodus 16-40, Leviticus, Numbers and Deuteronomy.

Just before the Israelites actually moved into the Promised Land, Moses warned them to keep God's Law. If they did, God would bless them in the land and protect them. But if they didn't, God would not bless them, and they would be at the mercy of their enemies. It's an ominous warning that comes at the end of Moses' life.

After Moses died, the Israelites finally moved into the Promised Land under the leadership of Moses' protégé, Joshua. The book of Joshua describes these events.

After taking up residence in the Promised Land, the twelve tribes of Israel lived in designated areas of the land. There was, however, no centralized government; the Israelites were led by local leaders known as judges. Some of the more well-known judges in the Bible are Samson, Gideon and Deborah. This period of time lasted for several centuries and is chronicled in the books of

Judges and Ruth. The very last line of the book of Judges sets up
the next part of the Old Testament story: *In those days Israel had
no king; everyone did as he saw fit* (Judges 21:25).

The next portion of the Old Testament story details the Israelite monarchy. Because the Israelites were surrounded by powerful enemies like the Philistines and Egyptians, they wanted to
be strong to deter any aggression on the part of their belligerent
neighbors. They viewed a king as a symbol of strength, so they
asked God to choose one. God cautioned them that asking for a
king was not wise, because kings would tax the Israelites, require
them to fight in wars, and generally make them his servants. Plus,
God himself was their king, and they were rejecting Him by asking for a human king. In spite of God's warning, the Israelites
persisted in their demand for a king. Because of their stubborn
insistence, God allowed a king to be chosen, and the centralized
Israelite monarchy began.

The first king was Saul, whom God eventually removed from
the throne because of his unfaithfulness. The next king was David,
a poor young shepherd who made a name for himself by defeating
the Philistine warrior, Goliath. David ruled around 1000 BC. David's son Solomon ruled after him and built a permanent temple
for God in Jerusalem. To find out more about these three Israelite
kings, read 1 & 2 Samuel, 1 Kings and 1 & 2 Chronicles.

After Solomon's rule, there was a dispute over who would suc-
ceed him, and Israel was divided into two nations: Judah (south)
and Israel (north). This was the political state of affairs for about
300 years, and this part of the story makes up a great deal of the
Old Testament. It's a sad period in the history of God's people
because it represents a cycle of disobedience. King after king, in
the north and south, was unfaithful to God—worshiping idols
and ignoring God's laws. Because of the kings' personal spiritual

failures, the Israelites also went astray. The prophets continually warned the kings and God's people to change their ways, but for the most part they did not listen. It was a downward spiral.

After centuries of patience, God followed through on the warning He gave to the Israelites prior to them taking up residence in the Promised Land. After generations of unfaithfulness to Him, God allowed the most powerful nations of the day to defeat the Israelites militarily and exile them from the Promised Land.

For the northern kingdom of Israel, this defeat occurred in 722 BC by the hand of the Assyrians. The southern kingdom of Judah lasted slightly longer before the Babylonians destroyed Jerusalem and the temple in 586 BC. After their defeat, the Israelites were exiled from the Promised Land. The Assyrians and Babylonians forced them to leave their homes and move east to Mesopotamia, a foreign land. There is a substantial amount of historical and archaeological evidence outside of the Bible that chronicles the defeat and exile of the Israelites. The divided monarchy and the exile are described in 1&2 Kings and 2 Chronicles.

The Old Testament story does not end here. In 539 BC, many of the Israelites began to return home from exile to the Promised Land. At this time, the Persians were the most powerful empire on the earth and they had a different type of foreign policy. The Persians did not insist on the exile of conquered peoples but instead allowed them to live in their homelands if they wished. God used the Persian Emperor, Cyrus, to allow the Israelites to return home. Cyrus even financed the rebuilding of the Jerusalem temple, which had been obliterated by the Babylonians. You can read about the return of the Israelites to the Promised Land in the books of Ezra and Nehemiah.

Now, let's recap the story of the Old Testament:

- Creation, early history of humanity

- Promises to Abraham; his descendants multiply into the Israelites
- Slavery in Egypt
- Israelites escape from slavery in Egypt
- Israelites receive the law and wander in the desert
- Israelites enter the Promised Land
- Period of the judges
- Period of the kings and pattern of disobedience
- Defeat by the Babylonians and Assyrians, Israelites exiled from the Promised Land
- Return of the Israelite exiles to the Promised Land

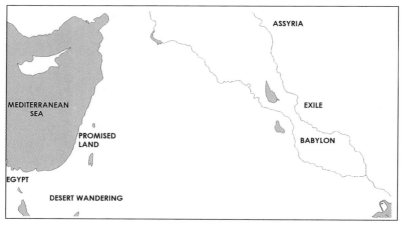

World of the Old Testament[7]

Structure of the Old Testament Designer Living is currently at the printer

As you may have noticed in the survey above, we did not cover all of the books of the Old Testament. So what about all the other books? What about famous books like Isaiah or Psalms?

How do they fit into this story? The answer lies within the types of literature in the Old Testament, and their arrangement.

The books of the Old Testament are not arranged in strict chronological order; primarily they are organized by genre. The historical books come first in the Old Testament, followed by Poetry, Wisdom Literature and the Prophets. You only have to read the historical books, Genesis through Esther, to get the overall story of the Old Testament. The rest of the books fill out that story with other types of literature.

For example, prophets were religious leaders that God used to speak for Him. Some of the more famous prophets included Isaiah and Jeremiah. These prophets were prophesying during the events recorded in the historical books. Let's look at the first verse of Isaiah: *The vision concerning Judah and Jerusalem that Isaiah son of Amoz saw during the reigns of Uzziah, Jotham, Ahaz and Hezekiah, kings of Judah* (Isa. 1:1). In other words, the prophecies that God gave to Isaiah occurred during the reigns of those four kings. You can read about those kings in the historical book of 2 Kings.

So the historical events associated with kings Uzziah, Jotham, Ahaz and Hezekiah are detailed in 2 Kings, and the book of Isaiah records what God was telling the Israelites during that time in history. You can read 2 Kings and Isaiah side by side. One of them is history, one of them is prophecy, but they both speak to the same part of the Old Testament story. This isn't obvious, though, because Isaiah is eleven books away from 2 Kings in the Old Testament. The fact that the Old Testament is structured according to genre explains how these two separate books can be related to each other.   Charts and suggested reading plans in the resource section further illustrate the structure of the Old Testament.

Active prophets during the divided kingdom and exile include Isaiah, Jeremiah, Ezekiel, Daniel, Hosea, Jonah, Micah and Habakkuk. Prophets who spoke after the Israelite return from exile include Haggai, Zechariah and Malachi.

Similar to the way that the prophets were writing during the events recorded in the historical books, other writings like the Psalms (Poetry/Songs) and Proverbs (Wisdom Literature) were written and compiled at various times throughout Israelite history. For example, Psalm 51 is a song of repentance traditionally attributed to David after he had an affair. Historical events found in in 2 Samuel 11-12 can be read alongside Psalm 51. The historical narrative of 2 Samuel and the poetry of Psalm 51 speak to the same circumstance, just in different ways.

To summarize, the Old Testament begins with Historical Narratives and Law, followed by a handful of books that are Poetry/Songs or Wisdom Literature. The last major chunk of the Old Testament is comprised of books of Prophecy. This means that reading the Old Testament straight through from beginning to end might not be the most effective approach, because it is not laid out in chronological order. It is organized by genre. See the chart of Biblical books on in the appendix for a summary.

A Strand of Hope

As previously mentioned, a huge part of the Old Testament could be characterized as a downward spiral. This is the period of the divided kingdom that led to the exile of the Israelites from the Promised Land. God was merciful and allowed the Israelites to return home, but it just wasn't the same. Decades had gone by, and they had to rebuild so many aspects of their former lives, including the city and temple of Jerusalem. There still remained the question of what God's relationship with humanity would look like. He had fulfilled his promise to Abraham and the Israelites were God's people, but they didn't really act like it. They were unfaithful. It was clear they could not hold up their end of the relationship.

But woven throughout all of that unfaithfulness and pain, we find a strand of hope. A promise for the future. We find prophecies about someone who will come one day to make things right. Someone who will finally restore life to what it was originally intended.

About 1,000 years before Christ was born, God made a promise to King David:

> *When your days are over and you rest with your fathers, I will raise up your offspring to succeed you, who will come from your own body, and I will establish his kingdom. He is the one who will build a house for my Name, and I will establish the throne of his kingdom forever. I will be his father, and he will be my son. When he does wrong, I will punish him with the rod of men, with floggings inflicted by men. But my love will never be taken away from him* (2 Sam. 7:12-15).

One day, God promised, a descendant of King David would sit on the throne and rule forever. God would be a father to Him, and He would be a son to God. Though He would be punished by floggings, God's love will never be removed from Him. This was the prophecy for the future eternal rule of one of David's descendants.

Several centuries later, the prophet Isaiah spoke this prophecy:

> *For to us a child is born, to us a son is given, and the government will be on his shoulders. And he will be called Wonderful Counselor, Mighty God, Everlasting Father, Prince of Peace. Of the increase of his government and peace there will be no end. He will reign on David's throne and over his kingdom, establishing and upholding it with justice and righteousness from that time on and forever* (Isa. 9:6-7).

A child would be born one day who would rule. He would be given great accolades and be called names that could only be applied to God. His rule would never end, and he would sit on David's throne. This is clearly the same person predicted in God's promise to David in the previous passage.

Here's another prophecy from Isaiah. See if this reminds you of anyone:

> But he was pierced for our transgressions, he was crushed for our iniquities; the punishment that brought us peace was upon him, and by his wounds we are healed. We all, like sheep, have gone astray, each of us has turned to his own way; and the LORD has laid on him the iniquity of us all. He was oppressed and afflicted, yet he did not open his mouth; he was led like a lamb to the slaughter, and as a sheep before her shearers is silent, so he did not open his mouth (Isa. 53:5-7).

This is one of the most remarkable prophecies related to Jesus. It describes a man who was punished on behalf of others. His wounds provided the way for us to be healed. All of our sin was laid on Him, and He went to His punishment willingly, without protesting. This prophecy was spoken centuries before Jesus was born.

There are countless other prophecies in the Old Testament that point toward the coming of Christ but we will end this quick survey with Micah:

> "But you, Bethlehem Ephrathah, though you are small among the clans of Judah, out of you will come for me one who will be ruler over Israel, whose origins are from of old, from ancient times" (Mic. 5:2).

This prophecy relates to that old familiar Christmas story. Mary and Joseph try to find a safe place for the birth of the Savior, and wind up in a stinky stable in the little town of Bethlehem.

DID YOU KNOW?

God's prophets constantly warned people about the foolishness of worshiping idols and sometimes openly mocked them for doing so! In 1 Kings 18, God's prophet Elijah has a showdown with the prophets of Baal, a false god that people worshiped with idols. Elijah and the prophets of Baal each agree to call on their own God to see which one answers. This showdown would finally prove which God was real (1 Kings 18:24).

When the prophets of Baal call on their god to show himself and he doesn't, Elijah begins to openly mock them. He suggests that maybe they're not yelling loud enough, or maybe Baal is just distracted by something else. He even says that maybe Baal is on a trip, or taking a nap (1 Kings 18:27)!

The prophet Isaiah got in on the action as well. In Isaiah 44:9-19, he points out how ridiculous it is for a man to fashion a little statue out of wood or metal, and then immediately bow down before it as if it's a god. He made it himself, and then he worships it – how dumb!

Group Discussion Questions

1. What has your view of the Old Testament been compared to your view of the New Testament?

2. Which part of the Old Testament story do you find the most interesting? The most confusing?

3. What does it tell you about God that He allowed the Israelites to be conquered and exiled? What does it tell you that He allowed them to return from exile later on?

4. What did you learn in this chapter about how the Old Testament is organized?

5. What stood out to you about the prophecies in the Old Testament that predict the coming of Christ?

6. What questions do you have about the Old Testament, and how do you plan on finding the answers?

5

A GLANCE AT THE NEW TESTAMENT

In the past God spoke to our forefathers through the prophets
at many times and in various ways, but in these last days he has
spoken to us by his Son, whom he appointed heir of all things,
and through whom he made the universe.
—Hebrews 1:1-2

When we flip the page in our Bibles from the last page of Malachi to the first page of Matthew, we are not only leaving the Old Testament behind and jumping into the New Testament, we are also entering into a completely new world. The world we left behind at the end of the Old Testament was radically different than the political and social situation that Jesus was born into.

At the end of the Old Testament, the Jewish people were slowly but surely returning to the Promised Land and picking up the pieces of their life before the exile. They were repairing the walls of Jerusalem and rebuilding the temple of God that

had been destroyed. All of this happened under the watchful eye
of the Persians, who ruled the known world about five centuries
before Christ was born.

So what happened between that time and Jesus' arrival? What
occurred in between the Old Testament and New Testament?
There are several centuries of history that are not recorded in the
Bible, and we know quite a bit about that time period through
ancient historical sources and archaeological evidence. This period
is known as intertestamental history, because it's the time period
that happened between the Old and New Testament.

Now I'm a history buff, so I love this kind of thing. But I
realize that not everyone is like me. You may not think of yourself
as a lover of history, but it really is important to have a sense of
what happened during this time. It helps to put what Jesus said
into context, and reveals the significance of what He and the early
apostles were saying against the backdrop of the broader culture.
I think you'll find that it brings the New Testament to life.

The intertestamental period was a time of major social change,
seismic shifts in political power, and large-scale warfare. It was
a time in which the Jewish people continued to cope with the
reality of being ruled by nations more powerful than themselves.
It's a period in which the Jews increasingly looked for someone to
come and deliver them – a savior who would rescue them from
the centuries of oppression they had endured. This tumultuous
period in history was initiated by a young king from Greece, a
man who had more influence on the world of the New Testament
than any other: Alexander the Great.

Around 330 BC, Alexander the Great conquered more ter-
ritory than anyone in history, taking over the entire Persian
Empire and establishing a dominion that stretched from Greece
to modern India. More important than his political and military

power was the *cultural* power he brought with him. It was like a social tsunami that followed his armies. The Greek language was spread throughout the Mediterranean world and the Middle East, as well as other aspects of Greek culture including philosophy, religion, literature, art, education, athletics, dress and architecture. Alexander the Great quite literally changed the world.

Theater and Temple of Apollo at Delphi, Greece (Photo by Ashley Lokkesmoe)

After Alexander died, the Greeks continued to rule his empire. The Jews later gained independence for a brief period after a rebellion against their Greek rulers, but ultimately they lost that independence when the Romans came to power in the century before Christ was born. The Romans were the most powerful and fearsome empire that had ever ruled over the Jews, and that dominance is seen throughout the New Testament.

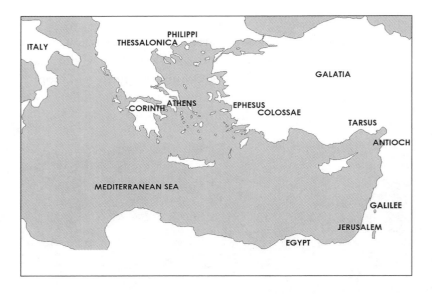

The World of the New Testament[8]

There is evidence of intertestamental history all over the New Testament. Here are just a handful of examples:

- Because of Alexander the Great, the vast majority of the Roman empire spoke Greek. This explains why the New Testament was originally written in the Greek language.

Greek inscription from the city of Ephesus

- Jesus' parents Mary and Joseph had to go to Bethlehem because of a census ordered by the Roman Emperor Augustus. This explains why Jesus was born there instead of in Mary and Joseph's hometown of Nazareth (see Luke 2:1-5).

- During his ministry, Jesus was questioned about the validity of paying taxes to Rome. Jesus' opponents questioned his loyalty to the Roman emperor (see Mark 12:14-17; Luke 20: 21-26; 23:1-2).

- Pontius Pilate presided over Jesus' trial and execution because he was the local Roman official (see Matt. 27:2; Mark 15:1; Luke 23:1; John 18:29).

- The apostle Paul was a Roman citizen, which afforded him certain legal rights and protections as he spread the gospel throughout the Roman empire. His legal status as a Roman citizen is highlighted several times in the book of Acts (see Acts 21:39; 22:25-29; 23:27).

- Paul founded churches in several cities that were fiercely loyal to Caesar, including Philippi, Corinth and Ephesus (see Acts 16:12-40; 18:1-19).

The intertestamental period shaped the world of Jesus' ministry and the environment of the early Church.

One of the main streets in Corinth, with shops on the right

Within the Jewish communities in Israel, there were significant social divisions. They had to cope with the reality of serving

Rome while trying to maintain their identity as God's people. Some Jews were comfortable with the Roman way of life, and enjoyed the luxuries associated with supporting the emperor. Others were militantly opposed to any cultural or military influence the Roman empire held over the Jewish people. There were various political and religious sects that included the Pharisees, Sadducees and Zealots. Each one had their own ideology and sense of what it meant to follow God and stay true to their heritage. For the Jewish people, it was a time of both external political oppression and internal social friction.

Jesus was born into this world of political and social turmoil— a world that was desperately waiting for a savior. It was perfect timing.

In Galatians 4:4, the apostle Paul says that God sent his Son into the world at the "fullness of time." The Roman empire at the time of Christ's birth was the perfect climate for His message. It was certainly a fullness of time in many respects. During that period, Greek was a universal language that nearly everybody could understand. The Romans had built roads that efficiently crisscrossed the empire. As a result, people traveled more than ever and information could be transmitted relatively easily. The Romans brought law and order to their empire, and people could move around from place to place with more security than ever before.

It was a world that was ripe for the spread of the gospel. People were hoping for a savior, and the message could spread easily. This is the world into which Jesus, the Savior, was born.

Structure of the New Testament

The first four books of the New Testament are the Gospels: Matthew, Mark, Luke and John. They cover the life and ministry of Jesus. Only Matthew and Luke include stories about Jesus' birth and childhood, but all four Gospels cover Jesus' ministry, arrest, trial, crucifixion and resurrection.

After the four Gospels, we have the book of the Acts of the Apostles (also just known as Acts). Acts is a historical narrative that covers the first thirty years or so of church history. It picks up right where the Gospels leave off, and shows how the Christian community grew from a relatively small band of Jesus' followers into a movement that spanned the known world.

The rest of the New Testament is comprised of letters written by various Christian leaders such as Paul, Peter, John and James. These letters were sent to Christian communities around the Roman empire, and they contain teachings about what it means to follow Christ.

Hebrews and Revelation are unique New Testament letters. Essentially, Hebrews is a sermon in letter form, and Revelation is a prophetic book about the future, written in letter form.

That's the basic breakdown of the New Testament: Gospels, Acts and letters. They cover Jesus' ministry, the growth of the church and the struggles those in the early church faced as they built new communities of faith in the midst of a culture with very different values.

The Four Gospels

Now that we have a basic understanding of the New Testament's arrangement, let's take a minute to understand what the Gospels are all about. It will help to put the next chapter on the Gospel of Luke into perspective.

As discussed in the introduction, the Gospels are a unique type of literature. They're kind of like separate biographies of Jesus. The Gospels are also full of historical narratives, with many sections of wisdom literature and prophecy embedded within them.

The Gospels were written by four different individuals at four different times in four different places. They cover the same subject matter and overlap in many ways, but each one has its own flavor. So why are there *four* Gospels? Why not just one of them? In the early years of the church, some people tried to combine all four Gospels into one long Gospel, but that effort was rejected by the church. It was agreed that there was something important about preserving all four of them as distinct voices—each one capturing something unique about Jesus and His ministry.

The best way to look at Matthew, Mark, Luke and John is to see them as four different perspectives on the same story. If you were to read the four Gospels one after another, you would get the impression that you're repeating information. You would also have the sense that each one is unique. That's because Matthew, Mark, Luke and John were telling the same story but in slightly different ways.

Let me explain it this way. I have one sibling, my younger brother Sean. He and I have the same parents, grew up in the same house and went to the same schools. We went on the same vacations, had many of the same friends, played the same sports and went to the same church. We share many of the same memories, and there is no one on earth who more closely shared my experience of growing up.

Let's pretend for a moment that Sean and I each decided to create a scrapbook of our childhood. He is going to make one, and I am going to make one. We're not exactly the scrapbooking type, but this is just a hypothetical scenario. Go with it.

Let's also say he and I have identical stacks of photos from our childhood that we will use to make these scrapbooks. We're working with the same materials. The pictures span the time period of our birth until high school graduation. We can arrange the photos and make the scrapbooks however we want, and we work independently. He doesn't know what I'm going to include, and I don't know how he is planning on making his.

I might look at all the photographs and decide that I'm going to lay everything out chronologically. I start with photos of my birth, and then infancy, and then all my pictures from elementary school. Next I would move into my middle school years and high school. I would include vacations in the year that we took them, and pictures related to sports and other activities in the appropriate years. It would be one seamless chronological story of my life. I wouldn't necessarily use all of the photographs to tell my story, however. I would only use the photographs that made sense with how I was organizing my scrapbook.

My brother Sean, however, might take a very different approach. Even though he is choosing from the very same photos, he might not be so concerned about chronological accuracy. He might want to lay things out *thematically*. So in his case, he might have a section on the different houses we lived in. He might have a section on birthday parties, or vacations. He might have a section on sports teams, or our family pictures. He would choose to include some things that I didn't even have in my scrapbook, and would omit some things I chose to include.

These two scrapbooks would look very different, but no one would suggest that we didn't grow up in the same house or that we didn't experience the same things. No one would suggest that mine was more accurate than Sean's, or that his was truer than mine. No one would suggest that because of the differences in our scrapbooks we can't know the truth about what it was like to grow up in our family. That would be ridiculous. It's the same story, told from two different perspectives.

This is what we have with the four Gospels: the same story from four different perspectives. They differ in structure, style, tone, content, but what's most remarkable are their similarities. They tell the same story.

Now that we have a basic understanding of the world of the New Testament and the nature of the four Gospels, let's dive into the Gospel of Luke.

DID YOU KNOW?

Jesus spent much of his time in the country, engaging with people who were on the poor end of the social spectrum. He preached primarily in Galilee, which was a rural area. Jesus was from Nazareth, a town in Galilee which had the reputation of being a kind of rural town.

In the countryside of Galilee, Jesus often taught the people in parables. It was a vivid and accessible way to bring His message. His parables were little stories that had meaning behind them. Each story got people to think, and they were full of images and scenes that were familiar to people who lived in the rural communities of Galilee. Many of the people coming to hear Jesus probably came straight from their own farms or walked through other farms to get to him.

When we look at the apostle Paul, it's a much different story. Paul spread the gospel and planted churches all around the Mediterranean world, and his ministry was primarily an urban one. He spent much of his time in large, strategic population centers like Corinth and Ephesus. He worked in crowded marketplaces and in the shadow of statues, temples, stadiums and theaters. Paul's letters are full of references to living and working in the crowded conditions of a large city.

Group Discussion Questions

1. Do you think it is important to have a sense of history when reading the Bible?

2. What does it mean to know that Jesus was born into a world of social and political turmoil?

3. Which part of the New Testament do you find the most interesting: Gospels, Acts, or letters?

4. What does it mean to you to know that the four Gospels are the same story told from four different perspectives? How will this affect the way you read Matthew, Mark, Luke and John?

5. What questions do you have about the New Testament, and how do you plan on finding the answers?

6

LUKE: MEET OUR SAVIOR

Today in the town of David a Savior has been born to you;
he is Christ the Lord.
—Luke 2:11

The Gospel of Luke begins with an explanation of purpose. The author writes his own introduction, and it's a very important set of verses. The first thing you'll notice is that Luke admits that he is not the first person to write a Gospel. He is not the first person who has sat down to write an account of what Jesus said and did. There were other Gospels out there, and Luke was about to add his to the collection that was already in circulation.

What and Why: Luke 1-4

Many have undertaken to draw up an account of the things that have been fulfilled among us, just as they were handed down to us by those who from the first were eyewitnesses and servants of the word. Therefore, since I myself have carefully investigated everything from the beginning, it seemed good also to me to write an orderly account for you, most excellent Theophilus, so that you may know the certainty of the things you have been taught (Luke 1:1-4).

In verse 2, Luke mentions his sources. His Gospel is based on information that he gathered from those who were "eyewitnesses and servants of the word." In other words, people who saw Jesus in action. Those who knew him, heard him teach and followed him. Eyewitnesses were the sources behind this Gospel, people who had been there "from the first." Luke wasn't talking to people who met Jesus late in his ministry. Luke based his Gospel on the testimony of people who were very familiar with Jesus and followed him from the very beginning of his ministry. They were in a position to provide the most accurate information.

In verse 3, Luke says that since he has "carefully investigated everything from the beginning," he thought it might be a good idea to write his version of the Gospel. He calls his version an "orderly account," which means that he has researched everything thoroughly and is going to lay it out in a logical, chronological, sequential order. In other words, what follows will be an accurate, historical portrayal of Jesus.

The next thing to notice is that Luke is writing this orderly account for someone he calls "most excellent Theophilus." Scholars debate the identity of this individual, but many have concluded that Theophilus was someone with significant power or influence. The Greek word that means "most excellent" is *kratistos*.[9] The only other times that Luke uses this word is when referring to Roman governors in the book of Acts (which Luke also wrote). So, it's probable that Theophilus – the man for whom Luke wrote his Gospel – was a public official or well-known figure.

So why would Luke write his Gospel for this man Theophilus? He tells us in the final verse of this rich prologue: so that Theophilus would have "certainty" about everything he had been taught about Christ. Theophilus needed encouragement about his new faith. He wanted to know more about Jesus and wanted to know why he believed the things he had learned. He wanted his faith to be rooted more deeply. Many of us have felt the same way, and we can all benefit from the Gospel of Luke just as Theophilus did twenty centuries ago.

This prologue tells us *why* Luke wrote this Gospel, and *how* he went about writing it. We get the picture that Luke was a meticulous historian or investigative reporter, interviewing eyewitnesses, digging for the truth and then laying it out in a coherent way. He provides this incredibly important information in the prologue, and it helps us have our bearings before we dive into the Gospel itself.

After the prologue, Luke begins his Gospel with the birth stories of both Jesus and Jesus' cousin, John the Baptist. Both were born under miraculous circumstances, and God had an important plan for both of them. Jesus is the Savior of all humanity, and John is the one who paves the way for His arrival. They were quite the dynamic duo.

We then read the familiar Christmas story of Mary's virgin birth, followed by a fascinating account of an adolescent Jesus talking confidently with the religious teachers in the temple.

In chapter 3, John the Baptist begins his preaching ministry, calling the people to repentance. Many people come to him to be baptized, including Jesus. At Jesus' baptism, the Holy Spirit descends on Him in the form of a dove, and God the Father says, "You are my Son, whom I love; with you I am well pleased" (Luke 3:22). Luke adds that the baptism happened when Jesus was "about thirty years old" (3:23).

In the beginning of chapter 4, Jesus is led by the Holy Spirit out into the wilderness where Satan waits to tempt him. For forty days, Jesus fasted and overcame the devil's temptations. Think about that for a second. Don't miss the amazing facts of this story. Jesus was out there in the desert for almost six weeks! He was praying and fasting under the blazing hot sun, coping with relentless hunger pangs and an ever-present craving for water. Not to mention Satan was taunting Him the whole time. Jesus' preparation for His public ministry was a long, arduous ordeal.

Afterward, the preparation is over. Jesus is ready to begin taking His message to the people directly, which he does in the next passage we examine.

Jesus Begins His Ministry: Luke 4:16-22

After being baptized and going into the wilderness for forty days, Jesus returns to Nazareth, his hometown, to start his ministry. Nazareth was not a metropolis; it was a relatively small town. Almost everybody would have known Jesus, and many of them would have known Him quite well. Jesus went into the synagogue, which was a local Jewish community center. On the Sabbath, they would have religious services that involved the reading of Scripture. With all that in mind, let's look at this passage:

He went to Nazareth, where he had been brought up, and on the Sabbath day he went into the synagogue, as was his custom. And he stood up to read. The scroll of the prophet Isaiah was handed to him. Unrolling it, he found the place where it is written: "The Spirit of the Lord is on me, because he has anointed me to preach good news to the poor. He has sent me to proclaim freedom for the prisoners and recovery of sight for the blind, to release the oppressed, to proclaim the year of the Lord's favor." Then he rolled up the scroll, gave it back to the attendant and sat down. The eyes of everyone in the synagogue were fastened on him, and he began by saying to them, "Today this scripture is fulfilled in your hearing." All spoke well of him and were amazed at the gracious words that came from his lips. "Isn't this Joseph's son?" they asked (Luke 4:16-22).

Did you notice in verse 16 that it says it was Jesus' custom to go into the synagogue on the Sabbath? He, like many of the other Jews in Nazareth, went to the synagogue on the Sabbath. So Jesus had probably read Scripture aloud many times before. It was part of His weekly routine. But this time it was different.

Luke writes that He took the Isaiah scroll, a book written 700 years before He was born, and read Isaiah 61:1-2. He read it, handed it back to the attendant and sat down like He had done many times before. But that wasn't it. With everyone still looking at Him, Jesus said something in verse 21 that He had never said before: "Today this Scripture is fulfilled in your hearing" (Luke 4:21). In other words: *I am the one Isaiah was talking about.* That was quite a claim. The silence must have been deafening.

Can you imagine the looks on the faces of everyone in that synagogue? Here was Jesus, the son of Joseph the carpenter, claiming to be the one that Isaiah had predicted hundreds of years earlier. Some people responded positively, but others began to ask the question, "Isn't this Joseph's son?" (Luke 4:22). They were essentially saying *Who does Jesus think he is?* People doubted Him from the very beginning of His ministry, and it was no different in His hometown. How could they go from thinking of Jesus as the young man who had always lived among them, to thinking of Him as God's Son or the Savior? For some people it was simply too much to accept.

Jesus chose the Isaiah passage intentionally. It's all about preaching good news to the poor and oppressed, and making sick people well. It paints the picture of a ministry that brings comfort to those found on the fringes of society: the poor, the sick, the blind and the powerless. The rest of the Gospel of Luke shows Jesus reaching out to these very people. Jesus is about to make the words of Isaiah come true.

It's important to take note of when Jesus, or any of the New Testament authors, quotes the Old Testament, because it often sheds light on the passage where the quotation is found.

BLURRY TIP

Pay close attention to quotations of the Old Testament found in the New Testament.

After this opening scene in Jesus' hometown, His ministry takes off. In the next several chapters, Jesus travels around Galilee and engages with all kinds of people. He performs healings, as well as popular miracles like the feeding of the 5,000 and the calming of the sea. He also offers some extended blocks of teaching, like the *Sermon on the Plain* in chapter 6. He also calls the twelve disciples and sends them out with power to work on His behalf.

Throughout this section (and the Gospel as a whole), we find different types of literature. Remember what we discussed in the introduction? The Gospels are a unique genre that combines various elements of other genres. Because of that, we have to vary our reading strategies as we go through them.

Some of this section of Luke is historical narrative; it's simply describing things that Jesus did and places He went. We can read those sections fairly easily and at a pretty steady pace. When Jesus starts teaching, however, we should slow down and really linger on what He's saying. In the Sermon on the Plain, for example, Jesus says, "If you love those who love you, what credit is that to you? Even 'sinners' love those who love them. And if you do good to those who are good to you, what credit is that to you? Even 'sinners' do that" (Luke 6:32-33). That's not something you want to just gloss over. It's important to slow down and ponder a teaching like this, so we can appreciate what Jesus is saying and think about how to apply it to our lives.

Remember that stoplight game we used to play when we were kids? Well, if you don't, here's how it goes. One kid is assigned to be the stoplight, and the rest of the kids line up like they're going to race. The kid who is the stoplight shouts out "green light!" and the kids start running. When the kid who is the stoplight yells "red light!" the other kids have to stop or they're out of the game. If the stoplight shouts "yellow light!" the kids have to walk instead of run. The "stoplight" continues randomly calling out red light, green light, or yellow light, and whoever makes it to the finish line first is the winner. It's a race, but the pace varies depending on what the stoplight says.

Reading the Gospels is kind of like that. There are some sections that are "green light" in the sense that you can just read them at a normal, steady pace. For the most part historical narrative is like that. Other sections require you to slow down or stop in order to understand what's going on or fully appreciate what is being said.

BLURRY TIP

Apply the stoplight strategy when reading the Gospels.

When we reach Luke 9:51, we hit a turning point. Previously, Jesus' ministry had been based in Galilee, the northern part of Israel, but that's about to change. Luke writes: *As the time approached for him to be taken up to heaven, Jesus resolutely set out for Jerusalem* (Luke 9:51). Jesus knew what was going to happen to Him. He knew He was going to die, and He moved toward His death willingly. He knew that Jerusalem was the place He would be arrested and eventually killed.

The next ten chapters are a steady march toward Jerusalem. It's a lengthy travel narrative that contains some of Jesus' most memorable teachings—many of which are told as parables.

A parable is a short story that has a meaning behind it, a moral that people can take away from it. Jesus told many parables. It was one of the most distinctive aspects of the way He taught. He would draw from everyday life and communicate truth in a way that was familiar and accessible to people. He talked about fig trees, vineyards, plants and seeds—all things that would be familiar to people living in an agricultural society.

Jesus also used people, institutions, and social groups to make His points, like the parable of the Pharisee and the tax collector found in Luke 18. Some of his most famous parables include the prodigal son and the good Samaritan—both found in this travel section of Luke. Let's take a look at the good Samaritan, which is probably the most famous of them all.

The Good Samaritan: Luke 10:25-37

As Jesus was on His way to Jerusalem, He interacted with a variety of people: men, women, Jews, Gentiles (non-Jews), rich people and poor people. He did not reserve His message for a specific group; He brought His truth for everyone. One of the people He famously interacted with was an expert in the law, a particular type of religious leader. This expert asked Jesus a couple of questions:

> *On one occasion an expert in the law stood up to test Jesus. "Teacher," he asked, "what must I do to inherit eternal life?" "What is written in the Law?" he replied. "How do you read it?" He answered: "'Love the Lord your God with all your heart and with all your soul and with all your strength and with all your mind'; and, 'Love your neighbor as yourself.'" "You have answered correctly," Jesus replied. "Do this and you will live." But he wanted to justify himself, so he asked Jesus, "And who is my neighbor?"* (Luke 10:25-29)

This man engaged Jesus on the topic of what it means to be saved, what it means to follow God. Jesus turned the question around and asked the expert what he thought the Bible said. The man answered, and Jesus said that he hit the nail on the head. But this expert wasn't finished. He wanted to know what it really meant to love your neighbor as yourself. So He asked Jesus, "Who is my neighbor?" Jesus replied with a parable.

When reading the parables or any other sections of Jesus' teaching, it's a good idea to understand the context. Who was Jesus speaking to? Was He speaking to a crowd or an individual? Was there a statement or situation that prompted Him to say what He did? Understanding the context helps us to know why Jesus said what He did.

BLURRY TIP

Pay attention to the context of Jesus' teaching.

The parable of the good Samaritan was Jesus' answer to the question about who qualifies as our neighbor. Let's take a look:

In reply Jesus said: "A man was going down from Jerusalem to Jericho, when he fell into the hands of robbers. They stripped him of his clothes, beat him and went away, leaving him half dead. A priest happened to be going down the same road, and when he saw the man, he passed by on the other side. So too, a Levite, when he came to the place and saw him, passed by on the other side. But a Samaritan, as he traveled, came where the man was; and when he saw him, he took pity on him. He went to him and bandaged his wounds, pouring on oil and wine. Then he put the man on his own donkey, took him to an inn and took care of him. The next day he took out two silver coins and gave them to the innkeeper. 'Look after him,' he said, 'and when I return, I will reimburse you for any extra expense you may have.' "Which of these three do you think was a neighbor to the man who fell into the hands of robbers?" The expert in the law replied, "The one who had mercy on him." Jesus told him, "Go and do likewise" (Luke 10:30-37).

You see, this parable is a brief story that has a point to it. It has meaning, which you might already be sensing after just reading it. The parable is meant to draw you in and get you to think about its lesson. Let's look at it a little more closely and then come back to what we're supposed to take away from it.

The man is described as traveling from Jerusalem to Jericho. Those two cities were relatively close to each other, and they were Jewish cities. So it's reasonable to assume that the man in this parable is Jewish. Along the way to Jericho, He is attacked, robbed and left for dead. This was pretty common back then, which is why people tended to travel in large groups rather than alone.

First, we read that a priest sees the man lying there, and how he deliberately walked by him on the opposite side of the road. The priest would have worked at the temple in Jerusalem, and was therefore also Jewish.

Next, a Levite walks by after seeing the man lying there and does nothing. Levites were Jewish men who worked at the temple in Jerusalem. That's two Jewish religious leaders that ignored the man lying in the road.

Finally, a Samaritan arrives on the scene and notices the injured man. He, unlike the priest and Levite, stops to help the man.

This act is significant because Samaritans and Jews did not like each other at all. They lived in close proximity to each other in Israel, but they had different views about God and how to worship Him. The relationship between Jews and Samaritans was full of social, political and religious tension, much like the friction between Israelis and Palestinians today. Jews and Samaritans wanted nothing to do with each other. Many Jews who were traveling from Galilee in the north down to Jerusalem in the south would take an extra-long route to avoid Samaria, the region where the Samaritans lived.

This social reality is on display in the Gospel of John as well. In that Gospel Jesus asks a Samaritan woman for some water, and this is her reply: "*You are a Jew and I am a Samaritan woman. How can you ask me for a drink?*" (John 4:9). John goes on to explain that Jews do not even associate with Samaritans.

Understanding the toxic relationship between Jews and Samaritans is essential to fully appreciating the parable of the good Samaritan. This is a perfect example of how some basic historical background can bring out the full significance of a passage. The easiest way to find this type of historical insight is to use a Study Bible. These Bibles provide valuable commentary on every section of the Bible. Study Bibles are great because you don't have to go look anything up. The work has already been done for you. Any historical or theological insight that's relevant to a particular passage has already been provided for you in the footnotes. It's like having a biblical scholar reading the Bible along with you.

BLURRY TIP

Use a Study Bible to easily find valuable historical and biblical insights.

So, it is incredibly significant that the Samaritan is the one who stopped to help the injured Jewish man. Not the Jewish priest or Jewish Levite, but a Samaritan man. Society would say that the Samaritan shouldn't care about the injured Jewish man. But this man did care. He helped the man at great personal expense to himself. He used valuable wine and oil to treat the man's wounds, and he paid for his hotel bill while he recovered. He paid with two "silver coins," which back then was the equivalent to two days of wages for an average worker. That's a lot of money for a stranger whom you probably don't like very much.

After sharing the parable, Jesus turned the question back on the expert in the law and asked him who he thought acted like a neighbor to the injured man. It's a rhetorical question of course, because the answer is obvious: the Samaritan. Jesus then tells him to do the same. That's what we're supposed to take away from the parable. We are supposed to do what the Samaritan did, which is to sacrificially help people when they're in need, even if we don't particularly like them.

I often hear people refer to helpful strangers as "Good Samaritans." While I understand why they use that term, the use doesn't do justice to the parable. The parable is not only about helping a stranger; it's about helping a stranger that you would rather not help. It's about helping someone at a significant cost to you. That's the definition of loving your neighbor as yourself—doing for them what you would do for yourself. That means extending them a great amount of grace and giving them the benefit of the doubt as we continually do for ourselves. It means being willing to serve someone when it's inconvenient or personally undesirable.

When reading the parables, it's a good idea to ask yourself how you are similar to the characters. Rarely are we similar to just one of them. We can be Samaritans in certain areas of our lives, and then quickly become the priest or Levite from this parable under other circumstances.

BLURRY TIP

When reading a parable, ask yourself how you are similar to each character.

After the extensive travel, Jesus finally arrives in Jerusalem. He drives out the corrupt money changers from the temple and begins to engage in debates with religious leaders who are not happy with Him and what He has been teaching. They also try to trap Him with political questions about the validity of paying taxes to Caesar, which foreshadows the accusations that will be made in His criminal trial.

Jesus offers a lengthy prophecy about the future of Jerusalem and the end times in chapter 21, and then Luke delves into the story traditionally associated with Good Friday. Jesus eats a last meal with His disciples before His betrayal and arrest. He is ultimately tried before the Jewish council and the Roman governor Pontius Pilate. Finally, He is beaten, humiliated, crucified and buried.

But that's not the end of the story. On the third day, Jesus broke out of the grave. He rose from the dead, and began to appear to His disciples and followers. The same people who watched Him die saw Him living and breathing again. Can you imagine what it would be like to watch someone die, witness his burial and then have him show up on your front door a few days later? I can't imagine. At the end of the Gospel of Luke, we get a glimpse of what a miracle of that magnitude would have looked like.

Jesus is Alive! Luke 24:36-49

While they were still talking about this, Jesus himself stood among them and said to them, "Peace be with you." They were startled and frightened, thinking they saw a ghost. He said to them, "Why are you troubled, and why do doubts rise in your minds? Look at my hands and my feet. It is I myself! Touch me and see; a ghost does not have flesh and bones, as you see I have." When he had said this, he showed them his hands and feet. And while they still did not believe it because of joy and amazement, he asked them, "Do you have anything here to eat?" They gave him a piece of broiled fish, and he took it and ate it in their presence. He said to them, "This is what I told you while I was still with you:

LUKE: MEET OUR SAVIOR

*Everything must be fulfilled that is written about me in the Law
of Moses, the Prophets and the Psalms." Then he opened their
minds so they could understand the Scriptures. He told them,
"This is what is written: The Christ will suffer and rise from the
dead on the third day, and repentance and forgiveness of sins will
be preached in his name to all nations, beginning at Jerusalem.
You are witnesses of these things. I am going to send you what
my Father has promised; but stay in the city until you have been
clothed with power from on high"* (Luke 24:36-49).

The disciples had a very authentic response to seeing Jesus
alive again. They were afraid! They were just sitting around talking
and all of a sudden, Jesus appears and says, "Peace be with you."
They all thought they had seen a ghost. Jesus knew what they
were feeling, and asked them why they were afraid.

The next several verses prove the reality of His resurrection.
Jesus let the disciples touch Him, and He asked them for some
food to eat. And He ate it right in front of them! It wasn't a ghost.
This was the same man they saw die a few days before.

But Jesus didn't come back just to prove He was alive. He
had a message for His disciples. He explained to them how His
death and resurrection had been foretold in the Old Testament
and how the good news of His message needed to be shared with
all nations. He then says that His followers are "witnesses of these
things." They have seen Jesus in action over the last several years,
and they can testify to the truth of what He has been saying. These
are the same eyewitnesses that Luke spoke about in the prologue
to the Gospel—the people who were His sources in writing it.
Jesus then finishes by instructing them to stay in Jerusalem until
they are "clothed with power from on high." I imagine they didn't
know what that meant at the time, but we read about it in Acts
2, when the Holy Spirit comes upon them and supernaturally

enables them to fulfill their mission.

The Gospel of Luke closes with Jesus blessing them and ascending into heaven. The disciples go back to Jerusalem, full of joy, and eagerly await the power that will be coming to them. In the next chapter, we will look at Ephesians, which is all about the new life that Christ offers us through His death and resurrection.

DID YOU KNOW?

Even Jesus' own disciples had difficulty understanding what He was teaching them. A great example is Jesus' miraculous feeding of the 5,000 in Mark 6. The disciples had only five loaves of bread and a couple of fish, and Jesus miraculously multiplied them to feed a crowd of over 5,000 people. Not long after that, in Mark 8, Jesus repeated the miracle and fed 4,000 people from just seven loaves and a couple fish.

You would think that the disciples would understand Jesus' power and desire to take care of people after seeing two miracles like that. Right after that, however, they were worried because they only had one loaf of bread. They were actually concerned about having enough to eat! Jesus rebuked them and asked, "Do you still not understand?" (Mark 8:21).

Even after spending several years with Jesus, it was hard to fully comprehend and apply what He was teaching. It's no wonder we struggle in matters of faith today, and with understanding the Bible. If you've ever struggled to understand the Bible, take comfort in the fact that Jesus' disciple Peter admitted that He himself had trouble understanding some of what was written in Paul's letters (2 Pet. 3:16).

Group Discussion Questions

1. How does viewing Luke as a meticulous historian affect the way you read his Gospel?

2. What was significant to you about the way Jesus kicked off His public ministry in his hometown of Nazareth? [See Luke 4:16-22]

3. What do you think about the stoplight reading strategy?

4. What did you find most interesting or challenging about the parable of the good Samaritan? (Luke 10:25-37) Which character(s) can you identify with? Why?

5. What did you notice about the disciples' reaction to seeing the resurrected Jesus in the flesh? (Luke 24:36-49)

6. Which *Blurry Tip* from this chapter did you find the most helpful, and why?

7. What questions do you have about the Gospel of Luke, and how do you plan on finding the answers?

7

EPHESIANS: EMBRACE THE GRACE

Three decades after Jesus was crucified and rose from the dead, the apostle Paul sat imprisoned in Rome, awaiting trial before Caesar. He had been wrongfully accused of breaking the law in Jerusalem, and was put on trial by the Roman authorities. Because Paul was a Roman citizen, he had the right to appeal directly to Caesar, which he did. That is how he ended up in chains in the capital city of the Roman empire. This fascinating account is found in Acts 21-28.

From his prison cell, Paul wrote several letters to churches and individuals. One of them was a letter to the church in Ephesus. We know it as Ephesians.

Greetings: Ephesians 1:1-2

Paul's letter to the Ephesians opens this way:

Paul, an apostle of Christ Jesus by the will of God, To the saints in Ephesus, the faithful in Christ Jesus: Grace and peace to you from God our Father and the Lord Jesus Christ (Eph. 1:1-2).

What do you notice about this opening? Can you tell that it's a letter? The first phrase (*Paul, an apostle of Christ Jesus...*) is the sender introducing himself to the reader. This is how the recipient would know that the letter is from Paul.

The next phrase, "*To the saints in Ephesus, the faithful in Christ Jesus*," tells us the addressees—the recipients of the letter. So this letter opens with the sender, and then the recipients. This was the standard form of letters in the first century.

The second verse (*Grace and peace to you...*) is the opening greeting. So the sender has been identified (Paul), as well as the recipients (the Ephesians), and an initial greeting has been offered. It's the ancient equivalent of an email that might open with something like, "Hey Tim, it's Ryan. I hope you're doing well!" Notice that Paul uses the word "grace" right there at the beginning. Keep that in mind because it's one of Paul's favorite words in this letter.

As you look at these opening two verses, what stands out to you? What questions do you have? When reading one of the letters, I find that it's helpful to do a self-interview. Pretend that you're interviewing yourself, and just ask some honest, open-ended questions about what you think the writer is saying. Remember the five W's of journalism? WHO, WHAT, WHERE, WHEN, and WHY. Those are classic questions that you can apply to much of Scripture, especially when you don't know where to begin. Every question doesn't apply to every passage, but it's a great place to start.

BLURRY TIP

Interview yourself about the passage.

In the case of Ephesians, you might not get past the first word of the letter. You might ask yourself, "WHO is this guy, Paul? I've heard his name before, but I really know nothing about him." Let's take a look at Paul.

The Apostle Paul

We have two main New Testament sources for Paul's life: The Acts of the Apostles, often called "Acts," and Paul's thirteen letters: Romans, 1 and 2 Corinthians, Galatians, Ephesians, Philippians, Colossians, 1 and 2 Thessalonians, 1 and 2 Timothy, Titus and Philemon.

Acts was written by Luke, the same man who wrote the Gospel of Luke. As we discovered in the last chapter, Luke was an early Christian historian who diligently collected and compiled as much information as possible about Jesus and His ministry and put it into his Gospel. But the Gospel of Luke is not all he wrote. Luke also wrote Acts as its sequel. Acts tells the story of the first thirty years of church history, and Luke spends significant time in Acts chronicling Paul and his ministry. Luke was a traveling companion of Paul's, so he had a front row seat for this exciting time in church history.

Paul's thirteen letters were written to churches around the Roman empire. He wrote them during the time period described in Acts. Paul would travel around the Roman empire, plant churches and then move on. After he left, he would send letters back to these Christian communities and function as their pastor via letter. You can read the historical narrative version of Paul's ministry in Acts, and then read what he wrote to these churches in his own letters.

Paul wrote his letters to encourage, teach, and in some cases, rebuke. In the midst of these letters, he revealed little tidbits about his background and biography. Together with what Luke describes in Acts, a picture of Paul the apostle emerges.

Paul was originally named Saul, and he was from a city called Tarsus on the southeast coast of present-day Turkey. Saul was from a Jewish family, though Tarsus was not a Jewish city. It was a very cosmopolitan place, and Paul probably spoke several languages including Aramaic, Hebrew, Greek and possibly Latin. Though Saul was from Tarsus, he spent a significant amount of his childhood away from home in Jerusalem, studying with a famous Jewish teacher named Gamaliel. Saul of Tarsus was a highly educated, well traveled, intelligent man.

As Saul got older, he stood out among his peers as especially knowledgeable and passionate about his Jewish faith. When Jesus and his crew hit the scene, Saul of Tarsus was not happy about it. He made it his mission to seek out and extinguish this new religion, which he saw as heresy. He obtained permission from the Jewish authorities to hunt down the followers of Christ and throw them in prison. These actions would haunt him for the rest of his life. In 1 Corinthians 15:9, Paul reflected on his past, writing, "I am the least of the apostles and do not even deserve to be called an apostle, because I persecuted the church of God."

One day, as Saul was on his way to Damascus to round up more of Jesus' followers, the risen Jesus suddenly appeared to him. Saul fell on his face. Jesus asked Saul why he was persecuting Him, and then gave him instructions about what to do next. Jesus had chosen Saul—the sworn enemy of Christianity—to be His "chosen instrument" to carry the gospel throughout the known world (see Acts 9:15).

Through the power of Christ, Saul of Tarsus left his anger, pride and self-righteousness behind, and became Paul the apostle—the greatest missionary the church has ever seen. You can read about his dramatic call in Acts 9. It's one of the most incredible passages in the entire Bible.

As you can imagine, the church was reluctant to trust Paul at first because of the way he persecuted them in the past. In time, he proved himself to the other disciples and church leaders, and he set out on multiple missionary journeys spanning thousands of miles and many years. He endured threats, beatings and all kinds of persecution in order to share the good news of Christ, though he would say the hardest thing was the constant anxiety he felt for all the new churches he planted and loved so much (see 2 Cor. 11:22-28).

Paul couldn't be everywhere at once, and all of the churches he established were under continual threat from both internal quarrelling and external persecution. It was very stressful for Paul to not be able to be present as these young churches faced such challenges. So, he did the only thing he could. He wrote them letters to teach and encourage them.

With that historical background in mind, let's go back to the beginning of the letter: *Paul, an apostle of Christ Jesus by the will of God, To the saints in Ephesus, the faithful in Christ Jesus: Grace and peace to you from God our Father and the Lord Jesus Christ* (Eph. 1:1-2).

So we know the WHO of this passage: it's Paul the apostle. He wrote the letter. But, if you keep reading, you might ask yourself, "WHERE is Ephesus?" or "WHAT was Ephesus like?"

These are great questions to ask, because they help us to picture the environment in which this burgeoning Christian community lived. Answering these questions can put Paul's words into context, which ultimately helps us to apply his words to our own lives in the 21st century.

Ancient Ephesus

If you were to visit Ephesus 2,000 years ago, you would find yourself in one of the largest and most important cities in the world; a flourishing metropolis of over 200,000 people on the western coast of present-day Turkey. Its strategic location on the sea and several major roadways made Ephesus an incredibly wealthy, prosperous city. The central feature of the city was the imposing temple of Artemis, one of the seven wonders of the ancient world. Artemis was a Greek goddess, and her temple in Ephesus was staggering. It was one of the largest buildings ever constructed up to that point in history and looked like a much larger version of the Parthenon in Athens. Its columns were over sixty feet tall! The structure would have been a jaw-dropping sight, even by modern standards.

People came from all over the Roman empire to worship Artemis at Ephesus. The locals were fiercely loyal to their goddess, which they made clear to Paul in a very tense incident described in Acts 19:23-41.

Ephesus was like any large, modern city of today. If the Roman empire could be compared to the United States, Ephesus would have been something like Chicago or Houston. Not the *most* populous city in the country, but among the largest and most influential.

Several years ago, I had the extraordinary opportunity to visit the site of ancient Ephesus in Turkey. It is one of the best-preserved ancient cities in existence today. I saw the massive theater that would seat 25,000 people for live performances, and walked the long marble streets where high-end goods and the latest fashions would have been sold. These streets were to Ephesus what Fifth Avenue is to New York or the Champs-Élysées is to Paris. Like any large and wealthy city, there were plenty of creature comforts, beautiful buildings, and signs of wealth.

Massive Ephesian theater built into the side of a hill

Marble Road, Ephesus

Ephesus also had the negative things that come with any large metropolis: poverty, high crime and a visible pleasure industry. On my visit to Ephesus, I saw a memorable example of this: an ancient business card of a local prostitute. Etched right into the marble street was a crude map to the brothel where this prostitute offered her services. It featured a portrait of the prostitute and a footprint that pointed the interested customer in the direction of the brothel, which was represented by a heart.

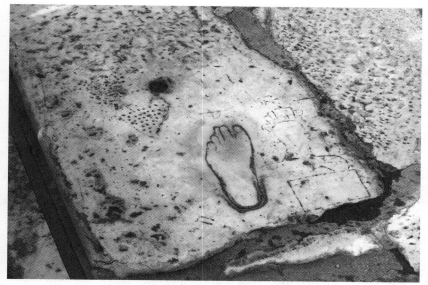

Brothel advertisement in Ephesus

Anything we can imagine happening in a large modern city was happening in ancient Ephesus. The recipients of Paul's letter were a very small band of new followers of Christ in a bustling metropolis dedicated to a pagan goddess. Their new lives could not have been more different than the lives of other Ephesians. That's what Paul was hoping for, in any case.

We have been spending a bunch of time on the first part of this letter. We're only two verses in at this point! That is intentional, because often there is important information packed into the beginning of Paul's letters. In fact, most genres in the Bible provide valuable information at the beginning, so it's worth spending extra time there no matter what book of the Bible you happen to be reading. Often we find background information or clues to the purpose of the book.

> BLURRY TIP
>
> Spend extra time on the beginning of any book
> you are reading.

Now we know a little bit about who wrote the letter, and a little bit about the environment of Ephesus. Let's see what Paul had to say in the rest of his letter.

What comes next in Ephesians after the initial greeting is a lengthy, passionate blessing in 1:3-14. Paul is using every poetic bone in his body, and he barely stops to take a breath! In fact, 1:3-14 is one long sentence in Greek—the language Paul used when he wrote the letter. This passage reveals how God has given us so many blessings in Christ, and how we were adopted as His children before the world was even created! Paul explains that we have been forgiven by grace, and that all of these blessings are guaranteed by the Holy Spirit. Frankly, this section can't be summarized easily—just go read it. It's one of the richest passages in the Bible.

Next, Paul expresses his thanksgiving to the Ephesians for their faith in Jesus, and shares how he prays for them (see Eph. 1:15-23). Paul often included a thanksgiving and prayer section in his letters after the initial greeting, and you can really sense his pastoral heart. We finally come to another passage that I'd like to look at in detail, which is all about our identity as Christians.

Dead or Alive? Ephesians 2:1-9

> As for you, you were dead in your transgressions and sins, in which you used to live when you followed the ways of this world and of the ruler of the kingdom of the air, the spirit who is now at work in those who are disobedient. All of us also lived among

them at one time, gratifying the cravings of our sinful nature and following its desires and thoughts. Like the rest, we were by nature objects of wrath. But because of his great love for us, God, who is rich in mercy, made us alive with Christ even when we were dead in transgressions—it is by grace you have been saved. And God raised us up with Christ and seated us with him in the heavenly realms in Christ Jesus, in order that in the coming ages he might show the incomparable riches of his grace, expressed in his kindness to us in Christ Jesus. For it is by grace you have been saved, through faith—and this not from yourselves, it is the gift of God—not by works, so that no one can boast (Eph. 2:1-9)

Just like we learned earlier to spend a little extra time at the beginning of any book in the Bible, it's usually a good idea to pay extra special attention to the beginning of a section or chapter. Usually you'll find a new topic introduced, or some new aspect to what is already being discussed. It often will summarize the section that follows, or introduce important themes.

BLURRY TIP

Spend extra time on the beginning of each chapter or section.

Look again at the first verse: *As for you, you were dead in your transgressions and sins.* That's what the whole first part of this section is about. We were dead before, because our lives were defined by sin. We weren't literally dead; our hearts were beating. But, we *were* dead in the sense that we had no hope for the future, and ultimately we would spend eternity separated from God because we had no way back to him.

Paul continues in the next two verses to explain what that dead life was like. Without a relationship with Christ, we walked in the ways of this world, a world which is influenced in large part by Satan—whom Paul refers to here as the "ruler of the kingdom of the air." This ruler, according to the passage, displays his power in those who follow him. Those who are disobedient.

According to Paul, we were *all* disobedient at one point. Disobedience defined our lives. What was that life like? It was dictated by the "cravings of our sinful nature." In other words, we just did whatever we felt like doing. It was an empty existence with no future and no hope. We were the "objects of wrath," just like everyone else on earth. We were people who would eventually face God's wrath for a life of disobedience and an unwillingness to admit our need for Him. That doesn't sound like a life that any of us would want.

But, God was not going to let things stay that way. By the way, the word "but" is one of the greatest words in the Bible. It's often followed by some wonderful news. Look again at the next section of our passage: "But because of his great love for us, God, who is rich in mercy, made us alive with Christ even when we were dead in transgressions—it is by grace you have been saved. And God raised us up with Christ" (Eph. 2:4-6).

You see, verse 4 begins with that great word: BUT. We were dead in our sins. We were on the same trajectory as a world that was desperate for God. We were ruled by Satan. We were living at the whim of our passions and desires. BUT...God intervened.

In God's rich mercy and love, He made us alive again with Christ. Did you catch that? God is merciful, and He *loves* us – deeply. More than we could ever imagine, He loves us. Think about the people you love the most in your life, and how deeply you love them. The love that you have for them doesn't even compare to how much God loves us! Because of His great love, He had mercy on us and made us alive again with Christ.

In the middle of verse 5, a very important word makes an appearance: grace. Paul is in the middle of talking about how we have been made alive with Christ, and he can't even contain himself. He just blurts out the phrase, "It is by grace you have been saved!" and then just continues on with his point. You see, grace is the most important word in the Bible, and the most important word in Ephesians.

Grace is undeserved favor. It's being treated well, despite the fact that you don't deserve it at all. It's different from mercy. Mercy is *not* getting what you deserve. It's withholding punishment or consequences. Grace goes a step further. With grace, not only do we *not* get the consequences we deserve, we are *given* blessings! That's what Paul is describing in this passage. Even though we were sinning—dead in our transgressions—God not only overlooked those offenses, He made us alive again with Christ! *That* is grace. Verse 6 says that we have been seated in heaven with Christ. It's a done deal. Through God's grace we have been made alive with Christ and our seat in heaven has been saved.

Paul continues by saying that we were raised with Christ and seated in Heaven with him "in order that in the coming ages he might show the incomparable riches of his grace, expressed in his kindness to us in Christ Jesus" (Eph. 2:7). In other words, one of the reasons that God saved us was so that for all of eternity we would be a monument to His grace and kindness. There will be all of these people seated in heaven with Christ, and everyone will know it was because of God's kindness and grace that they are there. That will be quite a scene.

By the way, did you notice in that verse that Paul used the word grace again? We've already seen it several times in just a few passages. In fact, Ephesians has the highest concentration of the word grace in the Bible (12 times in 6 chapters), and this won't be the last time we see it. Obviously grace is on Paul's mind, and his repeated use of the word demonstrates that it's a central concept he wants us to grasp in this letter.

The last two verses of this passage sum up what Paul has been driving at throughout all of chapter 2: "For it is by grace you have been saved, through faith—and this not from yourselves, it is the gift of God—not by works, so that no one can boast" (Eph. 2:8-9).

It's no surprise that these verses have been popular to memorize. Here, Paul uses the word grace again, and explains that our salvation is based on grace. Through our faith in Christ, we are saved by God's grace. Paul explains that grace is a gift, and that our salvation has nothing to do with our efforts whatsoever.

No one can brag about his or her salvation, because no one has ever contributed to it in any way! God is the only one who gets any credit for our salvation, because He saved us through His grace.

In the rest of chapter 2, Paul explains how God has united all people through Christ. Before Christ came, the Jews were God's people. Gentiles (non-Jews) were not part of God's people. In Christ, however, everyone has been brought together and included. The barriers have been removed. The invitation has been extended to all people, and all who are saved by Christ are fellow citizens in the household of God.

Paul uses architectural imagery to describe the house of God being built on the foundation of the apostles and prophets, with Jesus as the cornerstone. With all of the followers of Christ as part of the structure, the building comes together to be a holy temple of God.

In chapter 3, Paul reiterates that it was God's plan all along to include the Gentiles, and he prays again for the Ephesian Christians. This brings us to our next section that we'll examine in detail. But before we do, you might have noticed that we have been reading in longer sections. That's a great habit to get into, because reading in longer chunks helps provide the broader context of what you're reading.

> ## BLURRY TIP
> Read in longer chunks to understand the context.

A Worthy Life: Ephesians 4:1-6

As a prisoner for the Lord, then, I urge you to live a life worthy of the calling you have received. Be completely humble and gentle; be patient, bearing with one another in love. Make every effort to keep the unity of the Spirit through the bond of peace. There is one body and one Spirit—just as you were called to one hope when you were called—one Lord, one faith, one baptism; one God and Father of all, who is over all and through all and in all (Eph. 4:1-6)

The beginning of chapter 4 marks a very important transition in the letter. The first three chapters are primarily concerned with the nature of the Christian faith, and the new identity we have as Christ followers. Starting in chapter 4, Paul makes a switch and starts talking about what our lives should look like in light of what he said in the first three chapters. The letter takes a more practical turn, and Paul's tone is much more direct as he encourages his readers to behave in certain ways.

It's easier to notice this transition in some translations of the Bible than in others. In the original Greek, Paul uses the Greek word *oun* at the beginning of chapter 4, which clearly signals the change in direction. That Greek word oun is often translated as "therefore."[10] In the translation above, *oun* is translated as "then," which for some readers might not stand out as a major transition in the letter. This illustrates the value of reading multiple translations of the Bible, because each one brings out the various nuances of scripture as they translate from the original Greek and Hebrew. No one translation can do it all. Some of the more well-known translations are the NIV (New International Version), ESV (English Standard Version), and the NLT (New Living Translation). Each one has its own flavor, and they are all beneficial in different ways.

BLURRY TIP

Read multiple translations of the Bible to better grasp the full meaning of a passage.

It's very important to notice transitional words like "therefore" when reading the Bible. As my pastor growing up would say when he encountered "therefore" in the Bible, "You have to ask yourself, 'What is it *there for*?'" Often in Paul's letters, the word "therefore" appears right before he's going to encourage his readers to do something (or stop doing something). It's like the writer is saying, "Because of everything I just said…" Other important transitional words include *now, but, because* and *since*. They all are intended to focus your attention on what was being said before, and how it relates to what's coming next.

BLURRY TIP

Pay special attention to transitional words like *therefore, now, but, because* and *since.*

So, what is Paul hoping that we pay attention to in this first verse of chapter 4? Let's look again at what he said: *As a prisoner for the Lord, then, I urge you to live a life worthy of the calling you have received* (Eph. 4:1). Paul is strongly encouraging his readers to live their lives in a way that reflects the grace they have been shown by God. It's like Paul is saying, "OK, you've been saved by grace—that's great! Now, act like it."

In the next two verses (2-3), Paul lists some hallmarks of what it means to live a life worthy of our calling: humility, gentleness, patience, love—all bound together in unity by peace. If those qualities don't exist, then Paul would say his readers aren't living a life that is worthy of their calling.

He continues with the theme of unity for the last two verses of this section, using the word "one" seven times in verses 4-6. He says there is one body, one spirit, one hope, one Lord, one faith, one baptism, one God. Paul is driving home his point about unity by repeating the word "one" over and over.

Paul probably wrote this section to the Ephesians because he had heard that there was some disunity among them. Their different opinions were driving a wedge between them and jeopardizing the unity that God desires for them. You see, the ancient Ephesians were no different than we are today. All of the fractures and tendencies toward conflict or discord that we see in the present-day church were alive and well in Ephesus in the first century.

After this section, Paul continues with this theme of unity, explaining the variety of gifts that God has given to individuals in the church. All of the gifts play an important role and are designed to complement each other—not compete. He uses the image of the body with different parts working together to comprise a whole—with Jesus as the head (see Eph. 4:7-16).

Out With The Old: Ephesians 4:17-24

So I tell you this, and insist on it in the Lord, that you must no longer live as the Gentiles do, in the futility of their thinking. They are darkened in their understanding and separated from the life of God because of the ignorance that is in them due to the hardening of their hearts. Having lost all sensitivity, they have given themselves over to sensuality so as to indulge in every kind of impurity, with a continual lust for more. You, however, did not come to know Christ that way. Surely you heard of him and were taught in him in accordance with the truth that is in Jesus. You were taught, with regard to your former way of life, to put off your old self, which is being corrupted by its deceitful desires; to be made new in the attitude of your minds; and to put on the new self, created to be like God in true righteousness and holiness (Eph. 4:17-24).

Remember at the beginning of chapter 4, Paul encouraged the Ephesians to live a life worthy of their calling? When he comes to this section, Paul warns his readers *not* to live a certain way: *You must no longer live as the Gentiles do, in the futility of their thinking* (see 4:17).

Earlier when Paul talked about the Gentiles being included in God's church, he was talking about non-Jews who come to faith in Christ. In this passage, however, he's using the word "Gentile" in a different way. He is talking about the typical resident of Ephesus who wasn't Jewish, *and* hadn't come to faith in Christ. In this context, the word "Gentile" is like a code word for "non-believer." He is encouraging the Ephesians not to live as non-believers but to live noticeably different lives.

In the next two verses (18-19), Paul explains why the Ephesian Christians should not live like the typical non-believing Ephesians. These non-believers are "darkened in their understanding" and separated from God because of "the hardening of their hearts." They have "given themselves over to sensuality so as to indulge in every kind of impurity, with a continual lust for more." The marble advertisement for the brothel is a clear example of the Ephesian culture that Paul was warning his readers about.

Those who don't know Christ are on a completely different path. The non-believers in Ephesus are spiritually hard-hearted, and as a result, they do not understand what God has done for them, and are therefore alienated from him. The empty lives they lead is all about whatever feels good.

In Ephesians 2:1-9, which we reviewed earlier, Paul reminded his followers that they used to follow the way of the world and live for passions and the flesh—but that was before Christ! In this section, he is reminding them not to walk in those ways as the calloused, ignorant non-believers do. He's essentially saying, "Don't go back to your old ways! Everyone around you lives the way you used to. Don't be tempted to go back to that life!"

Paul summarizes the point in the final few verses of this passage. The Ephesians had been taught to "put off [their] old self," and to be "made new in the attitude of [their] minds." They knew the truth. Through Christ, they had been given a "new self, created to be like God in true righteousness and holiness" (Eph. 4:21-24). He then wraps up chapter 4 with some practical instructions on subjects such as honesty, anger, bitterness, slander, forgiveness and compassion.

Those who know Jesus, including the Ephesians reading this letter, have new lives and new selves. The old life, the old self, is dead. We have been re-created in the likeness of God, for the purpose of a righteous and holy life. A life that would please God. That's what this whole chapter has been driving at, which makes for a nice *Single Sentence Summary*:

CHAPTER 4: SINGLE SENTENCE SUMMARY

We should live our lives as a response to what God has done for us through his grace, and embrace our new identities given to us by Christ.

The remainder of Ephesians has more instructions for believers on how to be "imitators of God" (Eph. 5:1), and to walk as "children of light" (Eph. 5:8). Paul spends much of chapter 5 and part of chapter 6 talking about three socially unequal relationships of the first century world: wives and husbands, parents and children and slaves and masters. He gives guidance on the way these three groups should behave toward one another to preserve unity.

In the last part of chapter 6, Paul encourages his readers to take up the "full armor of God." The armor includes the belt of truth, breastplate of righteousness, shield of faith, helmet of salvation and sword of the Spirit (see Eph. 6:13-17). It's an incredible passage, full of vivid imagery and truth.

After some personal remarks and prayer requests in 6:18-22, Paul brings his letter to a close.

Signing Off: Ephesians 6:23-24

Peace to the brothers, and love with faith from God the Father and the Lord Jesus Christ. Grace to all who love our Lord Jesus Christ with an undying love (Eph. 6:23-24).

Paul has said what he wanted to say, and he is bidding his readers farewell. Notice how these verses are packed with themes we have seen throughout the letter: peace, love, faith and not surprisingly—grace. These words mean so much now that we have heard them defined and discussed throughout the letter.

The message of Ephesians might be summed up this way:

EPHESIANS: SINGLE SENTENCE SUMMARY

Because of his Grace, God made us alive in Christ so that we could live life in a way that would bring honor to God and reflect the great gift we've been given.

A great next step would be to go back and read the whole letter with all of this in mind. Remember, this is a letter—a *real*, ancient letter. It was originally intended to be read straight through. You wouldn't receive a letter in the mail and read it in twenty small pieces over the next month, would you?

I actually like to read Paul's letters three times in a row. The first time, I read it all the way through so I can get a sense of the overall tone and context. The second time, I slow down and read it in pieces so I don't miss any details. Some of Paul's letters are fairly complex, so it's best not to *only* read them in their entirety. After reading it slowly in pieces, I read it once more all the way through in one sitting. If you apply this technique, you'll be amazed how much more you will get out of any of the letters found in the New Testament.

BLURRY TIP

Read New Testament Letters three times in a row:
First, all the way through in one sitting.
Second, in small pieces over a longer period of time.
Third, all the way through in one sitting.

In the next chapter, we will look at the brief letter of James, which explains how to practically live out the new life that Paul talked about in this letter.

DID YOU KNOW?

People may have dozed off during the apostle Paul's sermons. Yes, he was the greatest missionary the church has ever seen. Yes, he probably gave stellar sermons in person. That doesn't change the fact that a long-winded sermon late at night will probably cause some people to drift off.

In Acts 20:7-12, a man named Eutychus dozed off during Paul's big farewell sermon and became famous for it. He didn't just fall asleep, he fell out of a third story window. It's a good thing Paul was there to raise him back to life!

Group Discussion Questions

1. How does knowing that Ephesians is a real, ancient letter affect the way that you read it?

2. Paul was a persecutor of the church. What does it tell you about God that he was willing to use a man like Paul to spread the gospel?

3. Did you find the historical information about the city of Ephesus helpful? If so, in what way(s)?

4. What are your thoughts about the differences between mercy and grace?

5. Can you think of an example of when you have been shown grace, or have shown grace to others?

6. What do you think are the biggest obstacles to living a worthy life—a life that reflects our new identity in Christ?

7. Which *Blurry Tip* from this chapter did you find the most helpful, and why?

8. What questions do you have about Ephesians, and how do you plan on finding the answers?

8

JAMES:
WORD TO THE WISE

James' letter is pretty remarkable. For most of his life, no one who knew him would have ever expected that he would write a letter like *this*. We don't know much about James from the time before he became the great leader of the church in Jerusalem, but we know enough to get a glimpse of the man.

We first meet James in the Gospels. When Jesus began His public ministry, He wasn't always accepted by those who knew him in His former life as a humble carpenter. It was just too hard for people to accept His claims. This was especially true in his hometown of Nazareth, which we saw earlier in Luke 4. After hearing Jesus teach in the synagogue, some of the people in his hometown weren't buying what He was saying. In Mark 6:3, they responded by asking, "Isn't this the carpenter? Isn't this Mary's son and the brother of James, Joseph, Judas and Simon? Aren't his sisters here with us?"

Here we learn that Jesus was from a family that was fairly well known in the area. People knew who Jesus' mom was, and who his brothers and sisters were. The first named brother is James, who was probably the oldest of Jesus' siblings. We assume this because he was listed first. That means that James was Mary's first child after Jesus. He was her first baby that was born under non-supernatural circumstances. James was Jesus' little brother.

We don't know how far apart they were in age, but James and Jesus probably had the typical relationship that most brothers have. James probably looked up to Jesus, and Jesus probably took care of James. Most likely, they played together and competed with each other. They knew each other better than anyone else. They were true brothers.

We can only guess what it must have been like to grow up in that house, but it's safe to say there was probably some sibling rivalry. James and his younger brothers and sisters probably heard the miraculous story of Jesus' birth many times as they grew up in Nazareth. They likely felt the mixture of emotions that most of us would feel: doubt, wonder, jealousy and frustration. They knew Jesus was special in some way, and certainly He seemed so in His mother's eyes. It's not a leap to think that it caused some tension in the family.

Additionally, it seems their father, Joseph, was no longer living. If he had been alive, he would have been mentioned in some way during the time of Jesus' ministry. His absence is very noticeable, and it probably means that he died some time during Jesus' youth.

There is also the fact that when Jesus was on the cross, He asked His disciple John to take care of His mother, Mary, after he was gone [John 19:26-27]. Apparently Jesus had been primarily responsible for her care up to that point, which strongly suggests that Joseph was no longer in the picture. If Joseph had been alive, he would have been responsible for Mary—not Jesus.

It is likely, therefore, that Jesus, James and their younger siblings had to cope with the pain of losing Joseph. Jesus, as the eldest son, would have stepped into the role of the head of the house. He would have been responsible for taking care of the family, and would have assumed a fatherly role with his younger siblings. It also may have been the case that James didn't always appreciate his older brother's efforts. What is clear, however, is that when Jesus finally began his ministry, his siblings did not believe His claims.

At the beginning of John 7, Jesus is trying to keep a low profile. His opponents are looking for an opportunity to kill him, so He deliberately avoids traveling anywhere near Jerusalem (see John 7:1). His brothers, including James, went to Him and said in John 7:3-5, "You ought to leave here and go to Judea, so that your disciples may see the miracles you do. No one who wants to become a public figure acts in secret. Since you are doing these things, show yourself to the world." The scripture goes on to say, "For even his own brothers did not believe in him."

His brothers did not follow Him. In this passage, they blatantly antagonized Him. They were taunting Jesus, saying something to the effect of "if you're so great, if you're everything that Mom always said about you, then why don't you just prove it?!" They couldn't accept that their brother was the Son of God.

On another occasion, Jesus' family tried to restrain him from continuing His work. In the Gospel of Mark, Jesus is preaching and performing miracles, and His family intervenes when it gets to be too much for them. Mark 3:2 says, "When his family heard about this, they went to take charge of him, for they said, 'He is out of his mind.'" Let's assume His family, including James, thought Jesus was crazy.

So how did James go from doubting his brother to following Him wholeheartedly? How did he go from thinking Jesus was crazy, to believing He was the Son of God? How is it that he ended up being the author of this letter in the New Testament? We have the answer, and it's found in 1 Corinthians 15. In this section, Paul is describing the historical events related to Jesus' death and resurrection. He writes,

> *For what I received I passed on to you as of first importance: that Christ died for our sins according to the Scriptures, that he was buried, that he was raised on the third day according to the Scriptures, and that he appeared to Peter, and then to the Twelve. After that, he appeared to more than five hundred of the brothers at the same time, most of whom are still living, though some have fallen asleep. Then he appeared to James, then to all the apostles, and last of all he appeared to me also* (1 Cor. 15:3-8)

Did you catch that? After Jesus came back from the dead, He appeared to His disciples and many other followers. But then He appeared to James by himself. James got a personal resurrection appearance. Wouldn't you love to be a fly on that wall? I'm sure that cleared up a few things.

Can you imagine what that must have been like? James was still mourning the death of His brother, and he probably may have felt some guilt about how he had treated Him. Then, all of a sudden, Jesus showed up. Any doubt that James had about Jesus' claims disappeared. He was probably terrified at first, and then filled with joy to see his brother again. Despite James' doubt, Jesus had a plan for him. He knew James' gifts, and he had a very important place for him in the ministry that was to come.

The next time we see James, he is the undisputed leader of the Jerusalem church. In Acts 15, James presides over a very important church meeting that includes the likes of Peter and

Paul. James, who had *not* followed Christ during his ministry, is now in a position of authority over some of Jesus' hand-picked disciples who *had* followed him.

James was one of the most influential early Christian leaders in the years after Jesus' resurrection. In 1 Corinthians, when Paul mentioned that Jesus appeared to James, everyone would have known who he was talking about. Paul didn't have to specify which James it was, because Jesus' brother had risen to such a high position of leadership.

This is the James that wrote the letter we will look at in this chapter: Jesus' biological brother and one of the giants of the early church. While Paul's letter to the Ephesians was all about our new identity as Christians, James' letter is about how that new identity plays out in our lives in a practical way. It's a much more pragmatic letter.

The Letter

Knowing everything we now know about James, it's astonishing to see how he opens his letter: "James, a servant of God and of the Lord Jesus Christ..." (James 1:1). Did you notice how he introduces himself? James doesn't play the brother card and mention that he grew up with Jesus. He doesn't brag about that. He doesn't view that as significant. For him, Jesus is not his brother; He's much more than that. He's the Lord, the one that he serves. That is the way he now views Jesus and the way he hopes his readers will view him.

In the rest of verse one, James addresses his readers: "To the twelve tribes scattered among the nations: Greetings"(James 1:1). So who are these twelve tribes? As you may remember, the Israelites in the Old Testament were divided into twelve tribes based on their lineage. Because of their history of being exiled and conquered, many of the Jews were scattered all over the known world, and large Jewish communities flourished in places like Rome and Ephesus. There were countless communities of God's people scattered around the Roman empire.

For James to say that this letter is addressed to the scattered twelve tribes is to say that he is addressing the letter to God's people living outside of Israel. He is writing to the Christian communities that are scattered around the Roman empire. In this sense, James' letter is much more general than many of Paul's letters, which were addressed to particular Christian communities in specific cities. James' letter addresses them all, and what he has to say would be applicable to all. He probably wrote the letter with the intention that it would be copied and circulated throughout the network of churches.

After the introduction, James launches into a section on enduring trials. At the time that James was writing, many of the early Christian communities were experiencing persecution because of their faith. The broader Roman world viewed the beliefs of early believers as a strange superstition. As a result, most Christians at the time faced persecution on some level, ranging from mockery to martyrdom.

Joy and Trials: James: 1:2-4

Consider it pure joy, my brothers, whenever you face trials of many kinds, because you know that the testing of your faith develops perseverance. Perseverance must finish its work so that you may be mature and complete, not lacking anything (James 1:2-4)

It's pretty amazing that James uses the word joy to describe trials. Imagine if you were reading this letter at that time in history. Maybe your sister had just been locked up for publicly reading the Scriptures. Perhaps your friend had been beaten by an angry mob in the streets. Does that seem joyful to you? For James, there is a joy to be found there, and he continues to explain why.

When trials occur, our faith is tested. It's not easy to keep faith when persecution or tribulation is part of our lives. When we are tested, our faith is made more secure, and produces perseverance for the future. It's like our faith is building up a callous; the trials hurt less and less as time goes on. Our faith can withstand so much more.

The result is that we would be "mature and complete," which has to do with *spiritual* maturity. When our faith perseveres through trials, we develop a spiritual steadfastness that leads us more and more toward maturity. James is telling us that even though the trials can be a very negative experience in the short run, in the end, they can produce a very positive effect in our lives. Because of this, we can find joy in trials.

As James continues his letter, we see right away that we are reading a letter comprised of wisdom literature. Not only is it full of practical tips on how to live a life that honors Christ, the subject matter changes quickly. There is no sustained argument or narrative as we often see in Paul's letters or other types of literature in the Bible. When reading wisdom literature, it's a good idea to slow down and ponder smaller sections, rather than just pushing through and reading a big block. It becomes monotonous, and it's hard to take it all in.

Also, when reading wisdom literature, notice when the subject changes. If an author is talking about being wise with money, and then all of a sudden the subject switches to something about family relationships, that's a good time to pause and really think about what he was saying about money before diving into the new section on relationships.

> ## BLURRY TIP
> When reading wisdom literature, pause whenever
> the subject changes.

After the section about enduring trials, James changes subjects and starts talking about faith and wisdom.

Double Minded: James 1:5-8

If any of you lacks wisdom, he should ask God, who gives gener-ously to all without finding fault, and it will be given to him. But when he asks, he must believe and not doubt, because he who doubts is like a wave of the sea, blown and tossed by the wind. That man should not think he will receive anything from the Lord; he is a double-minded man, unstable in all he does (James 1:5-8).

It's pretty clear that James is on a new subject at this point, leaving behind the brief discussion of perseverance through dif-ficult times. Here, James encourages his readers to simply ask God for wisdom. When James wrote this, he probably had Solomon in mind—one of the kings of Israel from 1,000 years earlier. After assuming the throne of Israel, God told Solomon to ask him for something. Solomon asked for wisdom, and God was pleased that he asked for this instead of riches or victory over his enemies. God granted Solomon's request and gave him a "wise and discerning heart" (1 Kings 3:12). James is encouraging his readers to make the same request of God.

But James doesn't just want them to ask God for something, he wants them to ask in a certain way. He wants them to pray and ask for this wisdom in faith, without any doubt. He wants there to be no uncertainty whatsoever in the request. He wants his readers to pray with confidence, knowing that God can answer the prayer, and wants to answer the prayer.

James then paints a picture to illustrate his point. The person who doubts when they are asking God for something is like a wave of the sea. Think about if you've ever been on a boat or near the shore when it's really windy. The waves are constantly thrashing around, crashing into each other. You can't predict exactly which way they are going to go. It seems completely random. As you scan the water and look to the horizon, it just looks like chaos.

That's what it's like for a person that prays with doubt. They shouldn't expect any answer from God because they don't really trust him. Their faith is not secure; it is being tossed around by the wind. James calls this kind of person a "double-minded man." This is a person that has a divided loyalty. They say that they believe in God and trust in Him, but they do not pray that way. The way they pray exposes their hidden doubts. This type of double-minded individual is unstable and haphazard with their faith, just like the waves of the sea.

After this, the subject changes, and continues to change. In fact, scholars have debated for centuries about the overall structure and organization of James. Some believe that there is more structure than meets the eye; others would say that it is just a loose collection of wisdom sayings. For most of us, it probably feels like the latter. That's why it's important to just take it piece by piece.

Hear and Do: James 1:22-25

In this next selection, James begins to touch on a subject that is a hallmark of this letter: the relationship of hearing the word (i.e. God's truth) and doing what it says.

Do not merely listen to the word, and so deceive yourselves. Do what it says. Anyone who listens to the word but does not do what it says is like a man who looks at his face in a mirror and, after looking at himself, goes away and immediately forgets what he looks like. But the man who looks intently into the perfect law that gives freedom, and continues to do this, not forgetting what he has heard, but doing it—he will be blessed in what he does (James 1:22-25)

In this passage, James encourages us to become doers of the word. For him, simply being a hearer of the word doesn't mean very much. In today's terms, James would probably say something like, "It doesn't mean much to go to church every Sunday if your life looks no different from Monday to Saturday."

James uses a vivid image to make his point. Someone who hears the word but doesn't do it is like a man who looks in the mirror, and then forgets what he looks like afterward. He gets a taste of his identity when he hears the word, but his life afterward doesn't change at all. The identity and life he is supposed to embrace is something he only hears about; he never puts it into action.

By contrast, the one who hears the word and actually makes changes in his or her life will be blessed. God didn't give us His word just for us to hear it and nod our heads approvingly. No, He wants it to take root in our hearts and affect every single thing that we do. That's the point James is making, and he's not finished with the subject. After touching on some other subjects briefly, he comes back to it in chapter 2.

Faith and Action: James 2:14-18

What good is it, my brothers, if a man claims to have faith but has no deeds? Can such faith save him? Suppose a brother or sister is without clothes and daily food. If one of you says to him, "Go, I wish you well; keep warm and well fed," but does nothing about his physical needs, what good is it? In the same way, faith by itself, if it is not accompanied by action, is dead. But someone will say, "You have faith; I have deeds." Show me your faith without deeds, and I will show you my faith by what I do (James 2:14-18)

This is one of the most well-known passages in James, and it has been a source of discussion and debate for centuries. It has to do with the relationship of faith and works. For many Christians, James' discussion of works in this passage is confusing, because, at first glance, it seems to contradict what we learned in Ephesians 2:8-9—that salvation is based on grace through faith. There is no contradiction, though, because James is not talking about how to be saved.

James is describing what our lives should look like as a *response* to our salvation. Salvation is free. It's a gift. Salvation is about what God has done for us, not what we do. The Bible makes that clear over and over again. But what should our lives look like *after* we are saved? That is the subject that James is tackling.

James uses pretty strong language in asking whether faith without works can save. What he *isn't* saying is that you have to do some good works to be saved. What he is saying is that if someone says they have faith, but their life looks no different than before, they should ask themselves if they really have faith. In James' view, an authentic faith will naturally yield a life full of good works. These works are not done *in order* to be saved, but rather as a *response* to being saved. If there are no good works, James wonders if you really do have a saving faith in the first place. If you have a saving faith, there should be good works as a result.

James gives the example of allowing someone who is in desperate need for food and clothing to remain that way, instead of helping them. James would probably say, "If you have a real, saving faith, then why wouldn't you help them?" He believes that good works are the proof of your faith. If your faith does not generate good works as a response to salvation, then that faith may not be authentic.

It's a very challenging section, because many people read this and feel like James is saying you have to do good works to be saved. He is not saying that. He is saying that an authentic, saving faith will naturally *produce* noticeable good works in our lives. If we say we have faith but there is no life change afterwards, James wonders if our faith is real. It's a challenging question that we all have to ask ourselves: what evidence is there in my life that my faith is real?

Taming the Tongue: James 3:3-5

In chapter 3, James begins to teach on the subject of controlling the way we talk. Here is an excerpt from that discussion:

> When we put bits into the mouths of horses to make them obey us, we can turn the whole animal. Or take ships as an example. Although they are so large and are driven by strong winds, they are steered by a very small rudder wherever the pilot wants to go. Likewise the tongue is a small part of the body, but it makes great boasts. Consider what a great forest is set on fire by a small spark (James 3:3-5)

Here, James uses three metaphors to describe the power in our speech. In the first case, he uses the example of a horse. Think about how powerful a horse is. It's one of the strongest animals out there, which is why it has been used for thousands of years for labor, transportation and in military battles. Despite their size and brute strength, horses can be controlled by the smallest bit in their mouth. A rider can tell the horse where to go and how fast to get there. It's the same way with our speech! Our heart and our whole lives will follow the direction of our tongues. The way we talk sets the tone for how we think and feel about things.

James uses a second example: a large ship being controlled by a rudder. Picture a huge ship on the open seas with its massive sails and large crew. It cuts its way through the water and withstands the constant battering of the wind and waves. Despite its size and power, one man can control it with one hand. The rudder is a relatively small piece of equipment when compared to the size of the giant ship, but even minor movements of the rudder can make a big difference in the course of the ship. It's the same with our speech. It controls our hearts and minds in a powerful way.

Lastly, James uses the analogy of a forest fire. He says that the great boastings of a small tongue is like a massive forest being set ablaze by a tiny spark.

So the whole point of this section is to share the wisdom in taming the tongue. If we keep our speech in check, we keep our hearts and minds headed on the right track. We have the potential to do significant damage if we don't tame our tongues.

If the Lord Wills: James 4:13-15

After covering some other topics, James comes to a section in chapter 4 about how we should view our lives and our futures.

> *Now listen, you who say, "Today or tomorrow we will go to this or that city, spend a year there, carry on business and make money." Why, you do not even know what will happen tomorrow. What is your life? You are a mist that appears for a little while and then vanishes. Instead, you ought to say, "If it is the Lord's will, we will live and do this or that"* (James 4:13-15)

James is pointing out the basic arrogance of assuming we will continue living our lives as we know it. We simply don't know how much time we have left here on earth because, as James says, we are only a mist. We are like fog that hangs around for a little while in the morning, and then just disappears as the day goes on.

His encouragement is for us to live our lives with that reality in mind. It should affect the way that we talk. We should be comfortable saying things like, "If God wants it to happen, we will move to that city" or, "If it's in God's plan, a new job will open up."

The Power of Prayer: James 5:13-16

Toward the very end of this diverse letter, James discusses prayer:

> *Is any one of you in trouble? He should pray. Is anyone happy? Let him sing songs of praise. Is any one of you sick? He should call the elders of the church to pray over him and anoint him with oil in the name of the Lord. And the prayer offered in faith will make the sick person well; the Lord will raise him up. If he has sinned, he will be forgiven. Therefore confess your sins to each other and pray for each other so that you may be healed. The prayer of a righteous man is powerful and effective* (James 5:13-16)

Whether things are good or bad, we should communicate with God. If things aren't going well, we should pray to God about it and let Him know our feelings and desires. If things are going great, we should tell God about it and thank Him through prayer and worship. Whatever the circumstances, we should not keep God out of the loop.

James then talks about the power of prayer. God can and does heal people through faithful prayers. James is calling his readers to take their prayers seriously and to pray with expectation when someone is sick. This is not a promise that every sick person will be healed every time, because as James said in the previous section, we should pray "if it is God's will. . . ."

Sometimes, it is not God's will for someone to be healed here on earth. We might not understand why, but we are not *supposed* to understand everything about God's will. We are not *able* to understand everything about God's will. He is God, and we are not. A man named Job learned this lesson in a very painful way but remained faithful to God. James actually praises Job as an example of steadfastness in the midst of suffering (see James 5:11). You can read about him in the book of Job, which is found in the Old Testament.

Whatever the case, the prayers of a righteous person, someone who is following Christ, are very powerful. James wants us to grasp this point.

A few verses later, James abruptly ends his letter. The five chapters that Jesus' brother wrote are a treasure trove of practical advice about living a life that honors Christ. He probably had a good idea of what our lives should look like because he had a front row seat to Jesus' perfectly-lived daily life. What James understood is that having a relationship with God is not simply about knowledge. God's truth compels us to live drastically different lives. That brings us to one more tip—a final question you should ask yourself after every time that you read the Bible.

BLURRY TIP

Ask yourself, "How can I apply this to my life this week?"

For example, after reading James you might ask yourself something like, "How can I tame my tongue this week? What practical steps can I take to make sure that my speech reflects my identity as a Christ follower?" Scripture is meant to be applied to our lives, so get in the habit of using this *Blurry Tip* as often as you read the Bible.

DID YOU KNOW?

All of the New Testament letters have very different tones. It's difficult at first to notice it, because it can often all just sound like "The Bible." Remember though, these are real, ancient letters, addressing a variety of situations. For example, Paul's letter to the Galatians is one in which he is furious over false teachings that have infiltrated that church. His tone is very blunt, and it's a letter filled with passion.

The letter to the Philippians, by contrast, is very friendly. Paul was apparently on great terms with the Philippians. Paul had a tumultuous, emotional relationship with the Christians in Corinth, so 1 and 2 Corinthians reflect that complex relationship. Letters like James and Romans seem less emotional by comparison, because they are written with a more general audience in mind.

Many of the letters also have a spoken quality to them, because it is likely that the New Testament authors dictated their letters to scribes who wrote them down. In a couple of cases, Paul actually goes out of his way to point out when he takes the pen and starts writing in his own hand. For example, in Galatians 6:11 Paul writes, "See what large letters I use as I write to you with my own hand!" In 2 Thessalonians 3:17, Paul writes, "I, Paul, write this greeting in my own hand, which is the distinguishing mark in all my letters. This is how I write."

Group Discussion Questions

1. What does it mean to know that James was Jesus' biological brother and that he didn't follow Christ during His ministry?

2. Have you ever experienced joy during trials, as James talks about in 1:2-4?

3. In what ways are we "double-minded" when we pray? (James 1:5-8)

4. What stands out to you about James' discussion of faith and works (James 2:14-18)? What did you find interesting or challenging about that section?

5. Which *Blurry Tip* from this chapter did you find the most helpful, and why?

6. What questions do you have about James, and how do you plan on finding the answers?

9

CORRECTIVE LENSES

Guard my teachings as the apple of your eye.
—Proverbs 7:2

Can you imagine a time in which Christians were killed if they did not turn over their copies of the Scriptures and renounce their faith? It happened. Can you imagine a time in which the church made it nearly impossible for average people to read their Bibles? It happened. Can you imagine a time in which millions of Christians were forced to worship in secret because of a constant threat of imprisonment or death? It happened—and it's happening right now.

In the early years of the church, Christians were persecuted regularly. Many people viewed followers of Jesus with suspicion and harbored all kinds of prejudices toward them. Every now and then, a man with absolute power decided to do something about it.

In the first century, the psychopathic emperor Nero decided to blame Christians for a fire that destroyed several neighborhoods in Rome. He rounded up as many believers as he could find and had them executed in horrific and public ways. His brutality was so extreme, the general public actually started to feel sympathy for the Christians they thought they hated.

A couple of centuries later, another Roman emperor named Diocletian attempted to extinguish Christianity: burning down churches, rounding up priests, torturing believers, and confiscating the Scriptures. Many Christians gave their lives to protect the church and the Scriptures, and their families had to watch them die publicly.

By the Middle Ages, Christianity had become the dominant religion in Europe, and the church had acquired tremendous political and financial power. Persecution no longer came from political authorities outside of the church. The threats were internal.

At that time, the only church-approved translation of the Bible was in Latin, which only the clergy and highly educated could read. As a result, most average Christians did not have direct access to God's word.

Then along came a German monk named Martin Luther. He *could* read Latin and concluded that the church had significantly distorted the gospel of Christ. He believed that personal faith in God is what mattered, and the ability to read the Bible for oneself was an important part of that.

In 1534, at great risk to his life, Martin Luther published the Bible in common German so that average people could read it. This was a revolutionary act. William Tyndale did the same thing in England, and in 1536, he was executed for it.

These new translations were published shortly after the invention of the printing press, which allowed them to be distributed very quickly. The revolution that Martin Luther sparked came to be known as the Reformation, and we all benefit from it to this day.

Today, millions of Christians face persecution in places like North Korea, Egypt, China and Iran. There are countless Christians in these countries who risk their lives on a daily basis to read the Bible and teach others about Christ.

God loved us enough to give us His word so that we can know Him better. Countless people throughout history have shed blood and tears for our ability to read the Bible, and we should never take that for granted.

Our Josiah Moment

Six centuries before the birth of Jesus, a king named Josiah ruled over Judah. He had become king when he was just a little boy, only eight years old. When Josiah was twenty-six years old, he decided that it was time to do some renovations on the Temple. He sent his administrators to begin work on the project, along with all of the various laborers that were going to do the physical work of restoring the Temple.

After the renovations began, some of the workers found a book. It wasn't just any book; it was the Book of the Law. It was God's Word. The workers gave the book to Josiah's secretary, who proceeded to read it to the king. Upon hearing its words, Josiah tore his robes, which was a sign of deep mourning. God's Word had been lost, or deliberately ignored, for generations. Josiah knew that neither he nor his people had been following what it said. There had been generations of disobeying and ignoring God, and Josiah was going to make some changes.

Josiah wasted no time. He brought the leaders of the people to the Temple, and he had the Book of The Law read to them. It was painfully obvious that they had let God down and hurt their relationship with Him. They didn't deserve any of His favor after centuries of disobeying him. So right then and there, Josiah and the leaders of the people pledged to follow God's Word with all their heart. They renewed their dedication to Him and removed all the idols and other tangible symbols of their collective disobedience.

Josiah had initiated an important reform—a return to knowing God and following His commandments. You can read about it in 2 Kings 22-23 and 2 Chronicles 34.

I believe the church is in need of a Josiah moment. We need to rediscover God's Word. We need to find it, dust it off and return it to its rightful place in our lives. We need to recommit ourselves to knowing and following God's Word, and we need to remove all other competition—because make no mistake, there is competition all around us.

There is competition every time we listen to music, turn on our TV's, read the news, check Twitter, or scroll through our Facebook feeds. There are influences all around us that constantly compete for our attention and allegiance in the very same way that the idols and false gods threatened the Israelites. If we allow ourselves to be overwhelmed by these influences on a daily basis, we passively allow God's Word to be pushed to the background. If that happens, we risk forgetting it entirely.

There are also voices that deliberately seek to discredit God's Word. They work to portray the Bible as something outdated and irrelevant. Those voices are becoming louder and more numerous with each passing day. With the invention of the Internet came the age of commentary and opinion. Many people have begun to view their personal opinions as the final source of truth. To them, if it's Bible vs. opinion, opinion wins.

Not so.

We need to rediscover God's Word and place it back at the center of our lives, where it can influence every thought, action and interaction we have. The simple first step in that process is committing to start reading the Bible. That's it. God's Word does not need to prove itself as valuable or true. If we simply start to read the Bible, its truth will be obvious. God's Word can speak for itself.

And in the End…

In Genesis, Luke, Ephesians, and James, we have learned the basic story of the Bible. God loved us and created us to be in a relationship with Him. When humanity sinned in the garden of Eden, that relationship was broken. Because of His great love for us, God was not content with things staying that way. He began to pursue humanity again through his promises to Abraham and His descendants, the Israelites.

As history unfolded, it became clear that we could not hold up our end of the bargain and maintain a healthy relationship with God. Sin still defined us. Drastic and permanent action was needed, so God sent His one and only Son, Jesus, into the world as our Savior. Christ paid the penalty for all of our sins, once and for all, and opened the door once again for a lasting relationship with God. We have been made alive through God's grace, and have been given new selves. Our old lives, our old selves, are gone. Our new lives, in all the day-to-day details, should now be lived as an ongoing response to the grace that God showed us through Christ.

That's the basic story of the Bible that we have learned through Genesis, Luke, Ephesians and James. But the final chapter hasn't played out yet. It has been written, but it hasn't happened. This is the chapter when Christ returns and ushers in a new and permanent era, a time in which sin and death are no longer a part of our lives. A time in which we have truly returned to the perfect relationship that God originally offered to us back in the garden of Eden.

This is the final chapter when "the Lord himself will come down from heaven, with a loud command, with the voice of the archangel and with the trumpet call of God, and the dead in Christ will rise first. After that, we who are still alive and are left will be caught up together with them in the clouds to meet the Lord in the air. And so we will be with the Lord forever" (1 Thess. 4:16-17).

This is also the chapter when humanity "will be [God's] people, and God himself will be with them and be their God. He will wipe every tear from their eyes. There will be no more death or mourning or crying or pain, for the old order of things has passed away" (Rev. 21:3-4). There are no words to describe what that will be like.

It is my hope that this little book has brought some clarity to the Bible and helped you in some way to discover, or rediscover, God's truth. It is my prayer that this discovery will lead you to a life of knowing and loving God, because He knew you and loved you long before you were born.

The grass withers and the flowers fall, but the word of our God stands forever. (Isa. 40:8)

Group Discussion Questions

1. What does it tell you about God that He gave us His word?

2. What does it mean to you to know that so many people have sacrificed to make the Bible available to you? How does this affect the way you read it?

3. What can we learn from the story of Josiah?

4. What are the greatest challenges to the Bible's authority in our lives?

5. What did you find the most interesting or challenging in this book?

6. What is the biggest takeaway for you after reading this book?

7. How do you plan on applying what you have learned in this book?

NOTES

1. "Blurry," *Merriam Webster Online Dictionary*, accessed August 13, 2014, http://www.merriam-webster. com/dictionary/blurry.

2. C.S. Lewis, *A Preface to Paradise Lost* (London: Oxford University Press, 1961), 1.

3. *The Ed Sullivan Show*, New York: CBS, February 9 1964.

4. Barclay Newman, *A Concise Greek-English Dictionary of the New Testament* (Stuttgart: Deutsche Bibelgesellschaft, 1993), 15.

5. Harry Gamble, *Books and Readers in the Early Church: A History of Early Christian Texts* (New Haven: Yale University Press, 1995), 49-66.

6. Dr. Roy Ciampa, various classroom lectures at Gordon-Conwell Theological Seminary, South Hamilton, MA, 2008-2009.

7. "Middle East,"accessed August 16, 2014, http:// d-maps.com/carte.php?num_car=596&lang=en.

8. "Eastern Mediterranean Sea,"accessed August 16, 2014, http://d- maps.com/carte.php?num_ car=3158&lang=en.

9. Barclay Newman, *A Concise Greek-English Dictionary of the New Testament* (Stuttgart: Deutsche Bibelgesellschaft, 1993), 103.

10. Barclay Newman, *A Concise Greek-English Dictionary of the New Testament* (Stuttgart: Deutsche Bibelgesellschaft, 1993), 129.

APPENDIX

RESOURCES

List of Blurry Tips

1. Single Sentence Summary.

2. When reading a poetic passage, slow down and picture it.

3. Pay attention to words and phrases that are repeated.

4. If a passage contains a list, write it out and number it.

5. When a passage reiterates or retells something from an earlier text, compare and take note of what is different.

6. Read actively by highlighting or underlining key words and phrases.

7. Pay close attention to quotations of the Old Testament found in the New Testament.

8. Apply the stoplight strategy when reading the Gospels.

9. Pay attention to the context of Jesus' teaching.

10. Use a Study Bible to easily find valuable historical and biblical insights.

11. When reading a parable, ask yourself how you are similar to each character.

12. Interview yourself about the passage.

13. Spend extra time at the beginning of any book you are reading.

14. Spend extra time at the beginning of each chapter or section.

15. Read in longer chunks to understand the context.

16. Read multiple translations of the Bible to better grasp the full meaning of a passage.

17. Pay special attention to transitional words like *therefore, now, but, because* and *since*.

18. Read New Testament letters three times in a row: First, all the way through in one sitting. Second, in small pieces over a longer period of time. Third, all the way through in one sitting.

19. When reading wisdom literature, pause whenever the subject changes.

20. Ask yourself, "*How can I apply this to my life this week?*"

CHART OF BIBLICAL BOOKS

Book	Primary Type(s) of Literature	Part of Biblical Story
Genesis	Historical Narrative, Prophecy, Poetry	Creation, Abraham
Exodus	Historical Narrative, Law	Escape from Egypt
Leviticus	Law	Desert Wandering
Numbers	Historical Narrative, Law	Desert Wandering
Deuteronomy	Law, Historical Narrative	Desert Wandering
Joshua	Historical Narrative	Promised Land
Judges	Historical Narrative	Period of the Judges
Ruth	Historical Narrative	Period of the Judges
1 Samuel	Historical Narrative	Period of the Kings
2 Samuel	Historical Narrative	Period of the Kings
1 Kings	Historical Narrative	Period of the Kings
2 Kings	Historical Narrative	Period of the Kings/Exile
1 Chronicles	Historical Narrative	Period of the Kings
2 Chronicles	Historical Narrative	Period of the Kings/Exile
Ezra	Historical Narrative	Return from Exile
Nehemiah	Historical Narrative	Return from Exile
Esther	Historical Narrative	Exile
Job	Wisdom Literature	N/A
Psalms	Poetry/Songs	Various
Proverbs	Wisdom Literature	N/A
Ecclesiastes	Wisdom Literature	N/A
Song of Solomon	Wisdom Literature	N/A
Isaiah	Prophecy, Historical Narrative	Period of the Kings
Jeremiah	Prophecy, Historical Narrative	Period of the Kings
Lamentations	Poetry/Songs	Exile
Ezekiel	Prophecy, Apocalyptic	Exile
Daniel	Historical Narrative, Prophecy, Apocalyptic	Exile

Hosea	Prophecy	Period of the Kings
Joel	Prophecy	Period of the Kings
Amos	Prophecy	Period of the Kings
Obadiah	Prophecy	Period of the Kings
Jonah	Prophecy	Period of the Kings
Micah	Prophecy	Period of the Kings
Nahum	Prophecy	Period of the Kings
Habakkuk	Prophecy	Period of the Kings
Zephaniah	Prophecy	Period of the Kings
Haggai	Prophecy	Return from Exile
Zechariah	Prophecy	Return from Exile
Malachi	Prophecy	Return from Exile
Matthew	Gospel	Life and Ministry of Jesus
Mark	Gospel	Life and Ministry of Jesus
Luke	Gospel	Life and Ministry of Jesus
John	Gospel	Life and Ministry of Jesus
Acts	Historical Narrative	Growth of the Early Church
Romans	Letter	Life of the Early Church
1 Corinthians	Letter	Life of the Early Church
2 Corinthians	Letter	Life of the Early Church
Galatians	Letter	Life of the Early Church
Ephesians	Letter	Life of the Early Church
Philippians	Letter	Life of the Early Church
Colossians	Letter	Life of the Early Church
1 Thessalonians	Letter	Life of the Early Church
2 Thessalonians	Letter	Life of the Early Church
1 Timothy	Letter	Life of the Early Church
2 Timothy	Letter	Life of the Early Church
Titus	Letter	Life of the Early Church
Philemon	Letter	Life of the Early Church
Hebrews	Letter, Sermon	Life of the Early Church
James	Letter	Life of the Early Church
1 Peter	Letter	Life of the Early Church
2 Peter	Letter	Life of the Early Church
1 John	Letter	Life of the Early Church
2 John	Letter	Life of the Early Church
3 John	Letter	Life of the Early Church

| Jude | Letter | Life of the Early Church |
| Revelation | Letter, Prophecy/Apocalyptic | End times |

THREE READING PLANS TO GET YOU STARTED

The following reading plans are meant to give you some concrete options of where to start. You've just digested so much information in this book, and these reading plans will give you plenty of opportunity to put what you've learned into action. Each of these plans focuses on a person or a period in history, and brings together multiple types of literature.

1. DAVID AND HIS SONGS

This plan looks at the life and reign of King David. Each reading pairs some historical narrative about his life with the Psalms which are traditionally thought to have been written by David. You will read about David in the historical narratives and hear David's own words in the Psalms. You can go through these writings at whatever pace works for you, but read in the order listed below. Remember not to rush through it, especially the Psalms. This reading plan could be completed in two to three months.

- 1 Samuel 16-17   Psalms 4, 5, 6, 7
- 1 Samuel 18-19   Psalms 8, 9, 11, 12
- 1 Samuel 20-21   Psalms 34, 13, 14, 15
- 1 Samuel 22-23   Psalms 52, 54, 63, 16
- 1 Samuel 24-25   Psalms 142, 17, 18, 19
- 1 Samuel 26-27   Psalms 20, 21, 22, 24
- 1 Samuel 28-29   Psalms 25, 26, 27, 28

- 1 Samuel 30-31   Psalms 29, 30, 31, 32
- 2 Samuel 1-2   Psalms 35, 36, 37
- 2 Samuel 3-4   Psalms 38, 39, 40, 41
- 2 Samuel 5-6   Psalms 53, 55, 56, 57
- 2 Samuel 7-8   Psalms 58, 59, 60, 61
- 2 Samuel 9-10   Psalms 62, 64, 65, 68
- 2 Samuel 11-12   Psalms 51, 69, 70, 86
- 2 Samuel 13-14   Psalms 101, 103, 108, 109
- 2 Samuel 15-16   Psalms 3, 110, 122, 124
- 2 Samuel 17-18   Psalms 131, 133, 138, 139
- 2 Samuel 19-20   Psalms 23, 140, 141, 143
- 2 Samuel 21-22   Psalm 144
- 2 Samuel 23-24   Psalm 145

2. EXILE AND RETURN

This plan covers God's people's exile to Babylon and the eventual return of the Israelites to the Promised Land. It brings together Historical Narrative, Poetry/Song, and Prophecy. This reading plan could be completed in one to two months.

- 2 Kings 24
- Jeremiah 21
- 2 Kings 25
- Lamentations 1-5

- Psalm 137
- Daniel 1-6
- Ezekiel 1-12
- Ezra 1-10
- Haggai 1-2
- Nehemiah 1-13
- Zechariah 1-14
- Esther 1-10
- Malachi 1-4

3. PAUL AND HIS LETTERS

This plan covers the life and ministry of Paul. It tells the historical narrative of Paul's ministry through the book of Acts and then brings in some of Paul's letters to the churches he was leading. You will read about Paul in Acts and read his own words in his letters. This reading plan could be completed in one to two months.

- Acts 7-9
- Acts 13-14
- Galatians
- Acts 16
- Philippians
- Acts 17
- 1 Thessalonians
- 2 Thessalonians
- Acts 18:1-18

- 1 Corinthians
- 2 Corinthians
- Acts 18:19-19:41
- Ephesians
- Acts 20-28
- Romans
- Philemon
- 1 Timothy
- 2 Timothy

BIG NAMES IN THE BIBLE

Below is a selection of important figures in the Bible, listed in order of appearance. There is a quick description for each individual, as well as a reference for the place in the biblical narrative where they first appear.

Adam	First man ever created, sinned in the garden of Eden	Gen. 1:27
Eve	First woman ever created, sinned in the garden of Eden	Gen. 1:27
Noah	Built an ark and survived the flood with his family and all the animals	Gen. 5:29
Abram (Abraham)	Chosen by God to be the father of the Israelites- the people of God	Gen. 11:26
Isaac	Son of Abraham and Sarah	Gen. 17:19
Jacob	Son of Isaac, his sons became the fathers of the twelve tribes of Israel	Gen. 25:26
Joseph,	Son of Jacob, sold as a slave to Egypt where he rose to prominence	Gen. 30:24
Moses	Led the Israelites out of slavery in Egypt and to the Promised Land	Exod. 2:2
Aaron	Moses' brother, priest of the Israelites	Exod. 4:14
Joshua	Moses' protégé, led the military conquest of the Promised Land	Exod. 17:9
Deborah	Prophetess and judge of Israel, battled Canaan	Judg. 4:4
Gideon	Warrior and judge of Israel, battled Midian	Judg. 6:11
Samson	A miraculously strong judge of Israel, battled the Philistines	Judg. 13:24

Ruth	Moabite woman who became the great-grandmother of King David	Ruth 1:4
Samuel	Prophet who anointed the first kings of Israel	1 Sam. 1:20
Saul	First king of Israel, later removed by God for his unfaithfulness	1 Sam. 9:2
David	Second (and most famous) king of Israel, defeated the giant Goliath	1 Sam. 16:11
Solomon	Third king of Israel, son of David, known for his wisdom	2 Sam. 12:24
Elijah	Miracle-working prophet, confronted the Israelites for their idol worship	1 Kings 17:1
Elisha	Miracle-working prophet, successor of Elijah	1 Kings 19:16
Josiah	King of Judah who initiated important religious reforms	2 Kings 21:24
Ezra	Priest who led Israelite exiles from Babylon back to Jerusalem	Ezra 7:1
Nehemiah	Leader who oversaw the rebuilding of Jerusalem after the return from exile	Neh. 1:1
Esther	Jewish wife of the Persian emperor, defender of the Jewish people	Esther 2:7
Job	A godly man who experienced immense grief and remained faithful	Job 1:1
Isaiah	Prophet of Judah, his prophecies are found in Isaiah	2 Kings 19:2 Isa. 1:1
Jeremiah	Prophet of Judah, his prophecies are found in Jeremiah	2 Chron. 35:25 Jer. 1:1
Daniel	Taken captive to Babylon, rose to prominence, had visions about the future	Dan. 1:6
John the Baptist	Prophet who preached about the coming of the Savior, baptized Jesus	Matt. 3:1
Mary	Jesus' mother	Matt. 1:16

Joseph	Mary's husband, Jesus' adoptive father	Matt. 1:16
Herod	Jewish king at the time of Jesus' birth, tried to kill the newborn Messiah	Matt. 2:1
Simon (Peter)	Leader of Jesus' twelve disciples	Matt. 4:18
John, Son of Zebedee	One of Jesus' twelve disciples, author of John, 1-3 John, and Revelation	Matt. 4:21
James, Son of Zebedee	One of Jesus' twelve disciples, part of Jesus' inner circle with John and Peter	Matt. 4:21
Matthew	One of Jesus' twelve disciples, former tax collector and author of Matthew	Matt. 9:9
Mary Magdalene	A well-known follower of Jesus, witness to Jesus' resurrection	Luke 8:2
Judas Iscariot	One of Jesus' twelve disciples, betrayed Jesus to the authorities	Matt. 10:4
Caiaphas	Jewish high priest, opponent of Jesus and his ministry	Luke 3:2
Herod Antipas	Jewish ruler of Galilee, opponent of Jesus and murderer of John the Baptist	Luke 3:1
Caesar Augustus	Roman emperor who exercised absolute authority over Israel	Luke 2:1
Pontius Pilate	Local Roman governor, presided over Jesus' trial	Luke 3:1
Stephen	Early Christian leader, the first Christian martyr in history	Acts 6:5
Saul (Paul)	Apostle who established and led many churches around the Roman empire	Acts 7:58
Barnabas	Early Christian leader, traveling companion of Paul	Acts 4:36
Mark	Cousin of Barnabas, traveling companion of Paul, author of Mark	Acts 12:12
Luke	Early Christian leader, traveling companion of Paul, author of Luke and Acts	Col. 4:14

Priscilla & Aquila	Husband and wife, co-workers of Paul, successful business owners	Acts 18:2
Timothy	Early Christian leader, Paul's protégé, recipient of 1-2 Timothy	Acts 16:1
Titus	Early Christian leader, one of Paul's co-workers, recipient of Titus	2 Cor. 2:13
Philemon	Early Christian leader, recipient of Philemon	Philem. 1:1
James, Jesus' brother	Former skeptic who became a key leader in Jerusalem, author of James	Matt. 13:55

PUBLICATIONS
Fort Washington, PA 19034

This book is published by CLC Publications, an outreach of CLC Ministries International. The purpose of CLC is to make evangelical Christian literature available to all nations so that people may come to faith and maturity in the Lord Jesus Christ. We hope this book has been life changing and has enriched your walk with God through the work of the Holy Spirit. If you would like to know more about CLC, we invite you to visit our website:
www.clcusa.org

To know more about the remarkable story of the founding of CLC International we encourage you to read

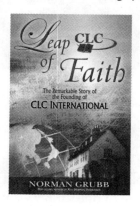

LEAP OF FAITH

Norman Grubb

Paperback
Size 5¹/₄ x 8, Pages 249
ISBN: 978-0-87508-650-7 - $11.99
ISBN (*e-book*): 978-1-61958-055-8 - $9.99

GETTING INTO GOD

Stuart Briscoe

Stuart Briscoe's *Getting into God* will take you through the basic elements of biblical study, prayer and witnessing. Whether you are a new Christian or one simply wanting to get back to the basics of your faith, this book offers some basic instruction on the "practicalities of Christian experience."

Paperback
Size 5¹/₄ x 8, Pages 144
ISBN: 978-1-61958-152-4 - $11.99
ISBN (*e-book*): 978-1-61958-153-1 - $9.99

RUNNING ON EMPTY

Jill Briscoe

Feeling burned out? Unfulfilled? Drained? Jill Briscoe offers hope and comfort for those times in life when we feel empty and tired. With wit and candor, Briscoe draws lessons from several biblical figures that provide spiritual refreshment and renewal to those who are *Running on Empty*.

Paperback
Size 5¹/₄ x 8, Pages 176
ISBN: 978-1-61958-080-0 - $12.99
ISBN (*e-book*): 978-1-61958-081-7 - $9.99

This book challenges us to leave casual Christianity behind and take God seriously, just as the prophets did!
Dr. Erwin W. Lutzer, Senior Pastor - The Moody Church, Chicago, Il.

Taking God Seriously
Major Lessons from the Minor Prophets

Stuart Briscoe

TAKING GOD SERIOUSLY

Stuart Briscoe

Seasoned pastor Stuart Briscoe examines each of the
Minor Prophets, providing both helpful historical context,
and demonstrating the relevance of each prophet's message to
believers today. If you want to take God's words from the Minor
Prophets seriously, this book will help enrich your Bible study.

Paperback
Size 5¹/₄ x 8, Pages 208
ISBN: 978-1-61958-078-7 - $12.99
ISBN (*e-book*): 978-1-61958-079-4 - $9.99

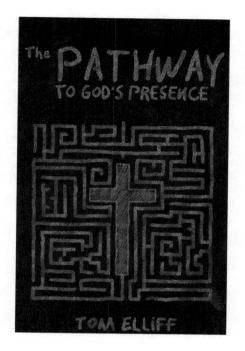

THE PATHWAY TO GOD'S PRESENCE

Tom Elliff

The Pathway to God's Presence encourages those who feel as though they have lost the sense of God's presence in their lives and wish greatly to restore it. Each chapter examines the Old Testament account of Moses and the often-wayward children of Israel, making clear the idea that "there is a distinct difference between God's provision and His presence."

Paperback
Size 4¹/₄ x 7, Pages 144
ISBN: 978-1-61958-156-2 - $9.99
ISBN (*e-book*): 978-1-61958-157-9 - $9.99